Cracked Mirrors

Allowing God to Destroy the Negative Self-Images in Your Life

TIARA CLOUD

Copyright © 2017 Tiara Cloud

Cracked Mirrors: *Allowing God to Destroy the Negative Self-Images in Our Lives*

ISBN-13: 978-0692988503 (For Such A Time)
ISBN-10: 0692988505

Unless otherwise stated, all Scripture quotations are taken from the Holy Bible, New Living Translation, copyright © 1996, 2004, 2015 by Tyndale House Foundation. Used by permission of Tyndale House Publishers, Inc., Carol Stream, Illinois 60188. All rights reserved.

Scripture quotations marked (NIV) are taken from The Holy Bible, New International Version® NIV® Copyright © 1973, 1978, 1984, 2011 by Biblica, Inc. Used by permission. All rights reserved worldwide.

Scripture quotations marked (ESV) are from The Holy Bible, English Standard Version® (ESV®), Copyright © 2001 by Crossway Bibles, a publishing ministry of Good News publishers.
Used by permission. All rights reserved.

Scriptures marked KJV are taken from the King James Version (KJV): King James Version, public domain.

Nature. (2017), Merriam-Webster, Retrieved from https://www.merriam-webster.com/dictionary/nature

Mirror. (2017), Merriam-Webster, Retrieved from https://www.merriam-webster.com/dictionary/mirror

*A special thanks and credit to contributing writers:
Juliette Bush, Tia Jones, Olga Meshoe, Roshanda Pratt.

All rights reserved. No part of this publication may be reproduced, stored in a retrieval system, or transmitted in any form or by any means, electronic, mechanical, photocopying or otherwise, without the prior permission of the copyright owner.

www.forsuchatime.today
ALL RIGHTS RESERVED
Printed in the U.S.A.

For bulk orders or other inquires, please email: tcloud@forsuchatime.today or visit: www.forsuchatime.today.

Dedication

I would like to dedicate this book to the man or woman who has allowed the reflections shown from the world's mirror to define their value and their worth. I pray you are encouraged as you are reminded over and over again of just how invaluable you are to God. It is also my prayer that you, as an image bearer of your Creator, wholeheartedly commit to seeking and trusting in His opinion of you. As you are comforted by His presence and reassured by His love, I pray that you arise, seek Him with all your heart and make the decision once and for all to passionately step into His purpose and will for your life.

Contents

Acknowledgments..9

Introduction..13

1. Cracked Mirrors: What Do You See?..................21

2. Grooming Our Insides.....................................37

3. Mirror, Mirror On The Wall..............................49

4. Letting God Clean Our Mirror..........................83

5. Our God of Peace..103

6. Reflecting Christ's Image................................121

7. For Such A Time..137

8. Using Cracked Mirrors....................................149

Helpful Resources..169

Acknowledgments

First and foremost, I dedicate this book to Father and Creator. Without Your love for me, Your patience with me and Your belief in me, and in Who you created, I would not have had the courage, strength or discipline to carry out this assignment.

To my Mother and Father, William & Rosetta Cloud, I want to express my sincerest thanks and love to you both for the love and sacrifice you have made for your children over the years. I appreciate all that you have contributed to influence me into the young woman I am today. **To my sister,** Angela Perdue: I love you very much sis, and I'm excited to see you riding high and walking in God's purpose for your life. Remember: the best is yet to come for you (Jeremiah 29:11). **To my big brother,** Steve Cloud, I love you very much as well. As always, I am praying for and rooting for you always.

To Pastor Robyn Gool and his wife, Marilyn: so very grateful to the gift that you are to the body of Christ. Your wisdom, love and heart for people goes only to show the great leadership that we have the opportunity of witnessing and learning from on a daily basis.

ACKNOWLEDGMENTS *(continued)*

To my sis-in-Christ and friend, Juliette Bush: Love you and appreciate you, sis! Thank you so much for your support from the beginning, and I'm grateful to God for the blessing of our friendship. I am so excited about all that God is doing and what He will continue to do in and through you. It's just the beginning!

To my dear friend, Wendy Chaplin: Grateful to God for our friendship over the years. I want to encourage you to step out into all that God has called you to. Don't settle!

To my VCCS Alumni & Friends Board Family *(Teresa Stanton, LeKisha Wheeler, Shasta Jenkins, Bill Tidwell, David Johnson and Aaron Johnson)*: Just wanted you guys to know that I love, appreciate and believe in each of you, and desire God's very best for you. I know that He will continue to bless you and provide you for the sacrifice you have made.

To my guest contributors: None of you hesitated when I asked if you'd share a portion of your testimony with the world, and I appreciate your support. Continuing to believe God with you that God will ultimately get the glory and that souls will be touched by it. Love each of you, and I know that God will continue to do great things in and through you. God bless you guys!

Cracked Mirrors

Cracked mirrors, refections of a fractured heart.
Lord, who do you see when you look at me?
I need a new start.
Blinded by the world's interpretation
of my worth, but you stepped in and restored
My tattered self-image first.
It all came together, my image became clearer.
I felt your love. I felt your love!
Once I stared in your Mirror,
My true value was revealed.
Not my own, but I bear your image,
I saw peace, I have joy, heart fulfilled.
My soul is well, Lord you're my Help
I will trust in you, I will rest in you.
Finally, my reflection is clear,
I'll stay near to your Mirror.

Introduction

Oftentimes, mirrors are symbolically linked to both the words reflection and introspection. In fact, the Merriam-Webster Dictionary defines the word mirror as a polished, smooth surface that forms images by reflection. They offer a true representation to its user. The funny thing about mirrors is that they can be either incredibly deceptive or extremely revealing, dependent on the psyche, vision and knowledge of the end user. Who can forget the infamous line: "Mirror, mirror on the wall, who is the fairest one of all?" coined from Walt Disney's popular movie Snow White and the Seven Dwarfs?

While most have heard of the main characters of Snow White, the dwarfs and the queen, many aren't aware of the fact that the entire story line was originally borrowed from a nineteenth century German fairytale "Little Snow-White" by the Brothers Grimm. The popular film simply borrowed

Cracked Mirrors

and expanded on this coined phrase. Nonetheless, in both renditions of the story, the scene leads to the same climax. In the fairytale, the queen of the land routinely goes to the mirror that she believes possesses some type of special power. "Magic mirror, on the wall - who is the fairest one of all?" Every day, she consulted with this mirror about the authenticity of her beauty and worth, and every day her affirmation is confirmed: "Then she was satisfied, for she knew that the mirror spoke the truth" (Remember this). To the queen's dismay, when Snow White came on the scene, the mirror's response changed to "You, my queen, are fair; it is true. But Snow White is a thousand times fairer than you." Her beauty, and in turn, her worth, was fleeting because it was always based on the appearance or existence of another.

Sadly, for centuries before and after the conception of this popular film and story, man and women have echoed the behaviors of the queen in the story of Snow White. Every day, they subconsciously consult with external sources to reveal their value within. How much time do we waste each day gazing religiously into the tainted glass of our phones and gadgets, seeking the ever-vacillating interpretations of self-worth that are sold to us by social media, magazines and Hollywood? In truth, society has been selling us faulty appraisals of our significance for

INTRODUCTION

some time now. Photo shopped magazine covers and social media posts deceive many into accepting an inaccurate view of themselves based on body image, social status or the opinions of others. Body shaming is at an all-time high; and unfortunately, we hear about the casualties of all of these shameful practices every other day.

THE HEADLINES READ...
*"Another teen commits suicide
because of extreme cyber-bullying."
"A celebrity accidentally overdoses from
a lethal mix of this drug or that."*

Whether or not we're aware of it, these tragic incidents have negatively affected the psyche of an entire generation. A generation who have fallen prey to the public opinion of a society that is simply unqualified to render much more than a faulty hypothesis on self-worth because they too are unaware of their own individual identities.

It's as if we're a part of one huge audition on one of those cheesy reality TV shows. The only difference is that in this audition called life, it is all too common for the millions of insecure individuals performing to spend hours of their time scrolling through social media pages or flipping through the latest fashion magazines to find out about the newest trending looks. Anxiously, they seek to gain the approval of others. They desperately wait to see if they made "the cut". "Did I make it?" "Am I acceptable now?" are so the questions they ask themselves subconsciously.

Truthfully, in all of us lies an innate desire to be accepted. We crave human acceptance and the desire to be loved, but if we're not careful, we can become so captivated by it that we are willing to forfeit our conscience, health, relationships and our entire identities just to obtain random caveats of validation from men and women not worthy to even be offering up their evaluations. If we are not careful, the mere concept of acceptance can become an idol in our lives.

God's love for us is like no other. There is no need for us to ever envy or be jealous of material things or the gifts and talents of others because He blessed us with our very own. He has created us each for a unique plan and purpose. Throughout this book, you will find a few, brief excerpts from the testimonies of individuals who've experienced first-hand God's transforming love. They too have battled with distorted self-image but have witnessed God's healing restoration in their lives. Maybe you'll even see a part of yourself in some of their stories. It is true that we were created in His image to honor Him and reflect His glory, but without Christ, mankind is doomed to simply be a massive pile of broken, juxtaposed glass…cracked mirrors

INTRODUCTION

no longer fit for the use of its Creator until we allow God to destroy our negative self-images and make us whole again.

THE ROUTINE

And so it begins. She pulls back the covers, rolls out of bed, turns on the lights then walks towards the cracked mirror on the wall opposite her bed. Over time, she's grown accustomed to ignoring the huge cracks down the right side of the mirror. She stares back intently at her distorted reflection, trying desperately to ensure that every hair is in place. Makeup – flawless. No wait! Just a bit more blush there and now, yes: **PERFECTION!**

The light chirp of her phone in the background interrupts her thoughts during her daily consultation with the mirror. Oh, faithfully deceitful, cracked mirror. Right on time. She quickly slides her finger across the shiny, glass face of her stylish new phone. Her notifications ought to be off the charts after that bangin' pic she took with the girls last night. Her dress was on fleek (insert current hip term for "absolutely fabulous"). She smiles, her pseudo-confidence soaring through the roof with every notification: 50, 75, 125! This gave her the high that she so desperately sought. "Yeeeeesss, girl! Work it!" She coasted into work, confident that all was right in her world. Today was going to be a good day.

An hour later at work, one of her fellow co-workers that she secretly both admired and envied, takes one look at her ensemble for the day (because she's secretly envious of her), looks her up and down disapprovingly and walks away. And just as quickly as the high of confidence rose — poof — it dissipates into oblivion, sending her into another downward spiral emotionally, until alas, she gets the next "high"...the one only obtained by gazing upon the sweet faces of shiny, glass gadgets and dirty, cracked mirrors.

Until tomorrow…

All Scripture is inspired by God and is useful to teach us what is true and to make us realize what is wrong in our lives. It corrects us when we are wrong and teaches us to do what is right. God uses it to prepare and equip his people to do every good work.
—**2 Timothy 3:16-17 NLT**

Cracked Mirrors: WHAT DO YOU SEE?

A *cracked mirror* is often associated with superstitious beliefs. In the occult, breaking a mirror is even said to bring 'seven years of bad luck' and that it was actually the Romans who created this false belief. The length of time of the misfortune supposedly came from the ancient, pagan Roman belief that it took seven years for life to renew itself. If the person looking into the mirror was not of good health, their image would break the mirror and the run of bad luck would continue for the period of seven years, at the end of which their life would be renewed, their body would be physically rejuvenated, and the curse would be ended.

Cracked Mirrors

To lay the proper foundation, it is important that we get a clear understanding of God's opinion of curses and occult world, as a whole. In Exodus 20:4-5 NLT, it says "You must not make for yourself an idol of any kind or an image of anything in the heavens or on the earth or in the sea. You must not bow down to them or worship them, for I, the Lord your God, am a jealous God who will not tolerate your affection for any other gods. I lay the sins of the parents upon their children; the entire family is affected—even children in the third and fourth generations of those who reject me."

It's pretty clear to see God's disdain for idolatry and the works of Satan. Originally, during the times of the Old Testament (before Christ), the Law or Torah dictated how God's people were to live. They lived a very strict and disciplined life as they structured their life to walk in obedience to it. It dictated how they interacted with each other and others and even how they ate. Upon further examination, some theologians and scholars actually argue that some of its instructions give further evidence of God's love for His people. They believe that some of the instructions given, particularly with their diet were actually protecting them by showing them how to best take care of themselves.

Goats, calves and other animals were regularly sacrificed to God for temporary redemption of the sins

WHAT DO YOU SEE?

of the people. However, when God sent His Son Jesus to earth, that all changed. In Galatians 3:13, it says, "But Christ has rescued us from the curse pronounced by the law." When He was hung on the cross, He took upon Himself the curse for our wrongdoing. For it is written in the Scriptures, "Cursed is everyone who is hung on a tree."

Once Jesus came to earth to die for our sins, He was made a ransom for us. Through His death, we received eternal redemption. What does that mean to us? It means that because of His sacrifice, we no longer have to make sacrifices of bulls and goats because through His blood we were set free and redeemed from sin and eternal death. We don't have to be concerned with being overtaken by evil things or people because God has given us authority to overcome the power of the enemy. If you are a believer, you have been redeemed from what the Bible calls "the curse of the law". In fact, these types of beliefs actually stem from the occult and contradict the very heart of God to give us a future and a hope.

"For I know the thoughts that I think toward you", says the Lord, "thoughts of peace and not of evil, to give you a future and a hope. —**Jeremiah 29:11**

In the verse above, God was speaking to the prophet Jeremiah, but because we have been adopted into the family of God, we are also privy to the same covenant. It is the heart of God for us, as followers of Christ, to uphold those promises in our lives. It is important that you get to know God for yourself, so that you know His opinion of you and what He has to say about the different circumstances we may be facing. His Word provides the road map for our lives. It doesn't matter what a preacher, friend, mom, dad, sister or any famous celebrity has to say about God. Be honest: do you really know Him for yourself? Why settle for a second-hand relationship with the Creator based on mere hearsay when you have the awesome privilege to have an intimate relationship with Him? The more you build and strengthen your relationship with God, the easier it will be to discern when we need to simply bring a negative thought under subjection (as we are encouraged to do in 2 Corinthians 10:5). This simply means that when we recognize that our thoughts are contrary to God's Word, we should identify the source, speak to those thoughts and command them to line up with God's Word. Negative thoughts and self-doubt do not have to rule your life. Pray to God for peace and for the faith and confidence to trust His Word no matter what.

At some point in all of our lives, we all have struggled with insecurity or doubt in some area of our lives or another. We've questioned the authenticity of a friend or family member's love for us. It's a wonderful thing to know

WHAT DO YOU SEE?

that we can rest assured in the fact that God's love for us will never change. Throughout the Word of God, we see the true character of God revealed. He desires good things for you and I, and it is His desire for you to have a hope for a bright future. Does that sound like the same type of God that would send curses or bad luck? Absolutely not. Our God is a good Father, and He isn't double-minded about our future or His desires to see us prosper, grow and mature in every area of our lives, especially spiritually. In Isaiah 54:17, we see that "NO weapon formed against" us prospers". This includes cults, curses and any other attacks from the enemy that dare to present themselves against God's children.

He genuinely loves and cares for us and once we are convinced of this in our hearts, it makes it easier to keep our faith in Him and resist trying to take things into our own hands. Though you may go through some trials and face challenges in life, always trust and believe that your future is safe in Christ.

IMAGE BEARERS

God is all-powerful and magnificent; there is none who even compares to Him. He is even the Creator of the concept of creativity, but it's important to note that, in contrast, the devil is not the creator of anything new. He simply resorts to trying to distort what God has already created for good. You may think this is being deep, but it's fact – one comparison could be the reference of the number seven by the occult, to reference bad luck when according to biblical scholars, the number seven is viewed as one of the sacred or holy numbers in the Bible. It is associated with completion, fulfillment and perfection. In similar fashion, our society is generally inundated with secular references to mirrors and self-reflection.

Satan is a defeated foe, and the words of our Father are far more superior to any ungodly doctrine of his or man. So now, if we can, let's dive on in and discuss the subject matter of mirrors beyond the superstitious undertones that the devil has endeavored to beguile us with. It's important that we examine the context in light of a far more superior Author and book: the Bible. As mentioned earlier, a mirror can also serve as a medium that light can reflect off of. As Christians, we are God's ambassadors here on earth, and the very same power that raised Jesus from the dead lives inside us. It is His desire that when people look at us, they see the reflection of one that has been touched by His love. The light of the love of Christ should radiate from the inside of us and penetrate the darkness around us (1 John 1:5). God loves us and wants us set apart for Him and for His use. These are desperate times in our world. There is so much that is going on in our world today and many are broken, hopeless and defeated. Those who do not know

WHAT DO YOU SEE?

Christ live in a dark world devoid of hope, they are looking for the light. They are looking for the answer that can only be found in Christ.

> [14] *"You are the light of the world—like a city on a hilltop that cannot be hidden.* [15] *No one lights a lamp and then puts it under a basket. Instead, a lamp is placed on a stand, where it gives light to everyone in the house.* [16] *In the same way, let your good deeds shine out for all to see, so that everyone will praise your heavenly Father.*
> **—Matthew 5:14-16**

If you do have a relationship with Christ, then you are the light referred to in the verse above. So many times, you may be tempted to be ashamed of letting the world know about our relationship with Christ, but we must realize that it's not about us. It's about the lost souls who are looking for the light that is reflected from you as a Child of the most High God. We are His representatives, and in all honesty, we may just be the only Jesus that some people have the opportunity to see, especially if they never walk through the doors of a church.

Just think about it: of all God's creation — the birds, trees, lions, insects, cats and dogs — we were given the unique privilege of being selected to be God's image bearers or mirrors on this earth. The account of the creation of mankind is given in Genesis 1. It says:

> [26] *Then God said, "Let us make human beings in our image, to be like us. They will reign over the fish in the sea, the birds in the sky, the livestock, all the wild animals on the earth, and the small animals that scurry along the ground." [27] So God created human beings in his own image. In the image of God he created them male and female he created them.* **—Genesis 1:26-27**

Did you get that? We are bearers of the image of the Almighty Creator. This is even more of a reason why, as followers of Christ, we should be motivated to love everyone and allow His love to shine through us. In addition to the importance of us sharing the Gospel and being called to love one another, a mutual respect for God's creation should prevent hate and malice from festering in our hearts. Remember: we hate the sin, not the person. (Side note: If you happened to pick up this book, and you have not yet established a relationship with Christ, know that He loves you so much and desires for you to turn your heart to Him. It doesn't matter how far off course you feel you have gone, it's absolutely no concern of His. He simply wants you back. If you're willing to give Him a try, you can stop right now and pray wherever you are or

WHAT DO YOU SEE?

simply flip to page 169 in this book for a sample prayer you can follow. Even if you feel that you are not yet ready, I invite you to stay with us to the end. I don't think you'll regret it.)

Whether you have accepted it or not, the fact is that you were created in God's image, in the likeness of the great, omnipotent Creator of the universe! No matter how others may view you and in spite of how you may even view yourself, God placed a high premium on you before you were formed in your mother's womb. In fact, you have such a high value in His eyes that in Genesis 9:6, He determined that the penalty for taking the life of one of His image bearers should be death.

> *Whoever sheds human blood, by humans let his blood be shed, Because God made humans in his image reflecting God's very nature. You're here to bear fruit, reproduce, lavish life on the Earth, live bountifully!*
> **—Genesis 9:6 The Message**

After the fall of mankind in the Garden of Eden, God was willing to give up His most prized possession – His Son Jesus – as a sacrifice so that we could be saved and brought back into right standing with Him. Do you see? He has already established your value and your worth, so lift your

Reflections of:

MS. JULIETTE BUSH: *31 year old young woman, serving as an executive assistant to a pastor in International ministry*

When you reflect on your image in the mirror, who do you see?
Someone who is still learning and growing, yet content with self

Summarize yourself prior to accepting Christ using 3 words:

Fearless • Adventurous • Focused

How does the viewpoint of the reflection that you see now differ from the person you were before your relationship with Christ? What's changed?
I feel like I have more attacks since my relationship with Christ but in a good way / perspective. I stand with confidence not just by my outer appearance but my inner man that seeps through. This is because I know my purpose, and the enemy tries to distract me. I have learned that tests and trials only build endurance. Before, I felt like there was a cap or a measurement point to knowledge/ wisdom. Now, I see, we will never "arrive," and are constantly on a journey.

What was one of the most influential events in your life that influenced your perspective now or your relationship with Christ, as a whole?

When I moved from New York to live in Dubai, UAE as a flight attendant. I was 7,000 miles away from home. I couldn't call up friends and family at the drop of a hat when I needed something or immediate advice. I had to depend on the Lord. When I lived in the states, I went to Bible Study and church each week to "get" the word. I never read the Bible for myself. However, when I was stripped away from all normalcies, I still yearned for community. I got a Bible I could read and understand (The NLT Life Application Study Bible) and began studying that each day and night. The words came alive. That is when my desires started to change, my perspective of life shifted, and my discernment sharpened. I then was discipled and found a local Bible-based church in Dubai. I was edified by community and did not "depend" on the pastor for the Word, but then I was able to have a relationship with Christ for myself and to be sharpened by what the preacher preached [during service].

How did God change your image? Share in three words:

Restored • Protected • Brave

head up high. God literally believed that you were *to die for.*

NEVER TOO LATE

It's paramount to bear in mind that even when we may feel broken and unusable for God's purpose because of hurt, rejection or failures, God is willing and more than able to mend the broken pieces of our heart, to restore our self-esteem and to make us whole again. In fact, He will restore us to a better condition than we were before because He loves us and so that He can use us for His glory! Maybe you've slipped up or totally abandoned your relationship with Christ. You've just been living life by and for yourself and now you find yourself contemplating having a relationship with Him. Well, regardless of where you may find yourself right now, please understand that your falling short or walking in sin can never change the fact that you are precious to God, any more than your diving into an ocean makes you a fish. No matter how far you feel you've run or strayed away and no matter what you've done, God is waiting with loving arms for your return. This is why I pray that you come to embrace the analogy of the mirror in your relationship with God.

When we envision a mirror, we are reminded of our reflection. We reflect on our self-image, on our competency and on the stigmas or statistics that we've allowed others to cast upon us relative to our reaching our true potential.

WHAT DO YOU SEE?

Our self-image epitomizes how we view ourselves in lieu of or in spite of our past triumphs or failures. Though it may be blemished, a cracked mirror doesn't cease to be a mirror because it becomes damaged; it simply morphs into a distorted reflection of what it was created to be until it is cleaned and renovated.

When we are faced with traumatic or disappointing situations in life or deal with betrayal and rejection, we often look outward to make a self-assessment of our worthiness inwardly. Unfortunately, this can easily become a severely damaging mental practice if we don't guard our spirit and protect our mental space. When our eyes are on those around us or fixed on the circumstances that we face instead of Christ, we become flustered and unsettled on our insides. Eventually, it just becomes commonplace to look to man for validation when defining our worth. This cycle is sure to ultimately lead to depression, discontentment and sometimes even strife when the desire for acceptance overpowers our desire to walk peaceably in the relationships we are engaged in. You have to be honest and ask yourself: "How closely netted is my self-esteem to simple, human triviality and opinions? It's amazing that, without God's healing power, rejection or neglect endured in a relationship even decades earlier can trigger pain or jealousy in a heart that seems so fresh, it feels as though the wound was just inflicted. Hurt or trauma from the past, whether wielded by others or self-inflicted, can often distort our self-image. God tells us that man is frail as breath (Isaiah 2:22), so don't allow yourself to become consumed with the opinions of man. Only Jesus succeeded in walking the earth, bearing God's image while perfectly carrying out the will of His Father. So, if we're going to be obsessed with anyone's opinion about us, it should be His! He can re-construct your fractured self-image and give you confidence when you've been weighed down by the pressures of this world.

Regardless of what stage of life that you currently find yourself, realize that God has given you unique gifts, talents and purpose. I want to plead with you not to short change yourself or forfeit your destiny because you failed to spend time with your Heavenly Father long enough to find out what His will is for your life, because you didn't take the time to sit in His face and just soak up His love for you. After all: He is our Creator, and who better for us — the creation — to go in order to properly understand our purpose and value than our Creator?

> *For if anyone is a hearer of the word and not a doer, he is like a man observing his natural face in a mirror; for he observes himself, goes away, and immediately forgets what kind of man he was. But he who looks into the perfect law of liberty and continues in it, and is not a forgetful hearer but a doer of the work, this one will be*

WHAT DO YOU SEE?

blessed in what he does. —**James 1:23-25**

In this verse, the apostle James compares God's Word (the Bible) to a Mirror. He encourages us and helps us to see that there is freedom and revelation in Christ and in the Bible, but we must be willing to accept what it reveals to us. God desires to show us through His Word **what manner of man or woman we are**. He loves us and accepts us the way that we are, but He loves us entirely too much to just leave us that way. He desires to transform you from the inside out, but will you let Him?

WHAT ARE YOU LOOKING AT?

Remember the story of the evil queen in the story of Snow White? The story goes, "Then she was satisfied, for she knew that the mirror spoke the truth." I am always fascinated by the countless references in Hollywood and other works of world literature over the centuries to the truths in the Word of God. When we look at God's Word, we receive a better understanding of Truth and righteousness (John 17:17). We are image bearers of God, and when we grow in our relationship with Christ, we are transformed from the inside out, and we become more like Him. In The Message translation, it expounds upon this fact by telling us that:

Cracked Mirrors

Whenever, though, they turn to face God as Moses did, God removes the veil and there they are—face-to-face! They suddenly recognize that God is a living, personal presence, not a piece of chiseled stone. And when God is personally present, a living Spirit, that old, constricting legislation is recognized as obsolete. We're free of it! All of us! Nothing between us and God, our faces shining with the brightness of his face. And so we are transfigured much like the Messiah, **our lives gradually becoming brighter and more beautiful as God enters our lives and we become like him**. *—2 Corinthians 3:16-18*

When we do take the time to reflect on God's Word, not only can we obtain satisfaction and more confidence in its validity, but we can also find wisdom. We can rest in the realization of what a good and faithful Father He is to us. The more we look to, depend on and trust in Him, the more we become like God, and our life journey becomes brighter and filled with purpose (Proverbs 4:18).

Grooming Our Insides

Hopefully, when you do look into the mirror on a daily basis, it's for the purpose of examining whether or not you need to make any adjustments to your physical appearance, including your face or clothes. Wouldn't it be pointless for you to spend time gazing intently into the mirror, notice that you need to wash the morning crud from your face, but instead of doing anything about your appearance, you decide to go skipping off merrily to your car and off to work or school? As ridiculous as that sounds, it best describes the daily routine of so many with the grooming of their spirit man. We are spiritual beings, we have a soul, and we live in a shell that we often refer to as body (1 Thessalonians 5:23). We are trained as children to take care of our outer shell and our minds, but since we are 3-part beings, it only stands to reason we should care of the whole man or woman, most especially our spirit man.

Even on days where we may be exhausted or just feel *blah* getting up in the morning, we know better than to only go to the mirror once a week to see how we need to make adjustments to our appearance, unless we want to be met with the awkward glances of our co-workers or loved ones. In the same regard, if we only take a look at the Mirror (the Bible) once a week on a Sunday, we really shouldn't wonder why we are stuck feeling overwhelmed or disconnected in our relationship with God, when Saturday rolls around. We contemplate how is it that I slipped in this area or that after we fall, when we didn't bother consulting God to see what areas in our lives we need to go to Him and seek His help about. How many countless moments in time per day do we spend looking into the mirror and our front-facing camera phone lenses to examine our appearance? **For the sake of our spiritual well-being, we have to be just as diligent about our spiritual grooming.**

Because God created us, He already knows us from the inside out. This is because we are His creation. He knows our gifts and talents and our weaknesses and strengths. He is already aware of our past failures or achievements. There is no part of your past that God is not already familiar with. When you spend time with the Lord or read His Word, are

GROOMING OUR INSIDES

you just simply going through the motions?

God's Word reveals truth to us, but when we don't meditate on it or seek Him to gain a better understanding on how it applies to our lives, it serves us no benefit. Just imagine an accomplished scientist holding the valve of a coveted anecdote to a widespread disease. Sitting at the opposite side of the table is a terribly sick man; the deadly disease has already started to run rampant in his body. He sweats profusely while he trembles there helpless and in pain. The scientist, anxious to bring relief to the suffering man, confidently places the valve on the table separating he and the ailing man. At that moment, the answer to his sickness is right in front of him in the valve. All that he has to do is grab it! But just imagine if instead of grabbing the answer, the sick man just starts to toy around with the valve itself, picking at the label. He holds up the valve towards the light, as he examines the contents of the bottle briefly, but instead of breaking the seal and consuming the anecdote, he opts to place the unopened valve back on the table in front of the scientist, as the disease continues to ravage at his body. Crazy, right?! Well, just as the valve contained the remedy to the man's disease and ultimately his death, Jesus is the accomplished scientist who holds the cure to all that is ailing us, spiritually, emotionally and physically. We have to desire to go deeper in our relationship with God and examine our hearts so that we can truly grow.

Cracked Mirrors

Regardless of how it may feel when you are seeking God's face in prayer, be patient. Wait on the Lord and be willing to just sit in His presence until you hear His voice. He will not forsake you or leave you helpless. God has given us the Holy Spirit to teach us the Word of God (John 17:17).

For a long time, I struggled with focusing in my devotional time with God. Just being honest: I have a creative mind, and at any given time, five different things can be going through my mind. It's a daily process of planning, concept creation, development and critical analysis that my brain goes through at the simplest of concepts oftentimes. In a work environment or even in some personal relationships, I've found my thought process to be beneficial. Other times…not so much. However, I have found more than ever the importance of turning off my brain and simply resting in God, of resting in His peace and His love for me. It wasn't easy at first, and I had to really pray for God's help, but eventually, the value of being able to just relax in God's presence was evident. You see, God gave us our intellects, and there is a time and place for them, but they serve of no use with spiritual matters. The Bible tells us not to lean to our own understanding but to trust God (Proverbs 3:5-6). After all, who developed our so-called intellects, the human brain and our psyche anyway? It's crucial that we develop such a heavy reliance on God that we exalt Him as Lord, both in our thought life

GROOMING OUR INSIDES

and in the actions that we carry out in our every-day lives. We have to be committed to buckle down and grow in our relationship with God. Through obedience and humility, we are able to see our lives genuinely transformed for God's honor and glory. So, don't be discouraged if your time with the Lord doesn't look or feel like someone else's. *Your relationship with God is special and unique*, and you have to figure out what works best for you.

For me, I sometimes may have worship music playing in the background while I start off reading or studying a certain topic that I may be dealing with at the time. Someone else may dance before the Lord while another may prefer complete silence during their devotion time. Don't put God or your relationship with Him in a box; He desires true fellowship with you. The more time you spend with Him and build your relationship, the more it is strengthened and the more you will hear and recognize His voice. So, don't give up – keep building your relationship!

WHO AM I?

In today's society, we are confronted with so many different narratives of the truth. I'm sure you've noticed that dependent on what news station you turn on, you may get two contrasting interpretations of one story. If you turn to your co-workers, family and even some friends, you will find that so many individuals cling so dearly to their truth. In some circles, the phrase "live your truth" is thrown around loosely in an effort to promote self-empowerment, but if we're really honest with ourselves, it also serves as a destructive form of humanistic philosophizing. What do I mean? Well, simply put: it often just excuses one's mistakes and any form of accountability that would affirm right from wrong. It attempts to put a feeble man or woman on the throne in place of the omnipotent Creator of the universe and all of mankind. This way of thinking is faulty, if not for any other reason, because when there is no right or wrong, one would have to reason, "Whose truth can really be trusted?" If my truth is in deep resistance or contrast to yours, which one of us is right? If one person's ideology is survival of the fittest, then is that individual wrong if they hurt or take what belongs to another? There must be a standard of Truth or else chaos, violence and injustice will abound reign supreme.

Through God's Word, we can obtain an untainted view of the Truth. We can see who we are in Christ and where we really are in our relationship with Him. We don't have to walk around confused about how we should view things or whether or not we are enough, because when we look to God, our value is clearly defined. He literally thought you were to die for. He desires for you to prosper in life, so He'll make it clear what areas we need to seek His help in. It's comforting to know that we don't ever

GROOMING OUR INSIDES

have to worry about whether or not God's love for us will fade because of failures or past mistakes. Sometimes, we can become disheartened when others devalue our worth based on their perception of us or past failures. Well, sis / bro I want to encourage you, by reminding you that even when we've allowed cracks to form in our self-image, it's never too late to refocus in God's Mirror. His Word is our Mirror, and it is unchanging (Hebrews 13:8); it will stand forever (Isaiah 40:8). That simply means that God's love for you is a constant one that you can always rely on. Unlike the opinion of the mirror to the queen in the story of Snow White, God's opinion of you will never waver.

Man's opinions of us can be fickle and literally teeter-totter from day to day because of insecurities, immaturity, unforgiveness, jealousy, hate, and the list goes on — but not God's. His opinion of you will NEVER change. He loves us, and will always tell you the truth. You can take His Word to the bank!

SELF-IMAGE

For so many years in my life, my self-image was based heavily on what others thought of me and how they treated me from day to day. If someone decided that they didn't want to speak to me or simply just didn't like me, I'd literally go back and rack my brain trying to figure out why. Why didn't they like me? What did I do or not do? I was so hard on myself, and I struggled greatly with accepting God's opinion of me. I have often put certain individual's personal preferences or opinions of me in a position that only Christ should have been. They may have just been having a bad day, but if they took any of it out on me, I took it as a personal assault on me or my character. And some of those times, I found out later that it was really someone who simply didn't care for me, the way I did things or my personality, as a whole. It happens, but talk about living in complete and utter bondage. I was definitely always the more soft-spoken one, always the one to try to be the peacemaker in the situation but, God had to toughen me up. I had to learn and grow past that all -- and I'm still growing to this day. Of course, little by little, I started noticing that the more I took a stand on certain issues or simply expressed opinions that contrasted with someone else, I quickly found out just who was for me and who wasn't. With the help of God, this forced me to really evaluate the authenticity of certain friendships and relationships. Renowned poet, author and civil rights activist Maya Angelou once coined the clever phrase "When someone shows you who they are, believe them the first time." In the same regard, the Holy Spirit's opinion is far more superior then any mere man's. He began to draw me closer to Him and His Word to "test every spirit" (1 John 4:1). His Word gives us insight that we will know a person

GROOMING OUR INSIDES

by their fruit, so we don't have to live in a constant state of confusion and disappointments. He blessed me with godly friendships where I could receive both encouragement and constructive criticism when needed to.

God cares about each and every aspect of our lives. Did you know that it is God's desire for you and I to have a healthy self-image? The Bible states in Proverbs 23:7: "As a man thinks in his heart, so is He." How many times have we all gone through the same routine as the lady at the beginning of the chapter? We naively settle for the skewed evaluation of our significance based on the opinions of others. I want to encourage you to reject the lies that the enemy has sold you about your value and worth. For so many, more likes on social media equate to more validation; more compliments equal acceptance and approval; more money equals better social status, which inevitably equals more worth and so on. We are created in the very image of God! However, if we are not regularly reflecting on the Word – our Mirror – it is easy to fall into the routine of haphazardly evaluating our worth based on the opinions of our peers and other insignificant sources.

INSPECTING YOUR CONFESSION

Did you know that in addition to your obedience and trust in God, faith is activated by your confessions? In Matthew 12:34-37, Jesus says:

Cracked Mirrors

³⁴ You brood of snakes! How could evil men like you speak what is good and right? For whatever is in your heart determines what you say. ³⁵ A good person produces good things from the treasury of a good heart, and an evil person produces evil things from the treasury of an evil heart. ³⁶ And I tell you this, you must give an account on judgment day for every idle word you speak. ³⁷ The words you say will either acquit you or condemn you."

Our words are powerful. Our thoughts influence the words that come out of our mouths, and what we continue to say, we eventually will act out. *Words frame our world.* Making positive confessions over your life, that line up with what God's Word says is not about denying the physical facts surrounding any circumstances you may be facing; it is about exalting God's Word above all else and reflecting on what the Mirror tells us about the circumstances of our lives, and how we should think, speak and react. This principle is also evident when discussing the gift of salvation. In Romans 10:9-10, it tells us that, *"⁹If you confess with your mouth the Lord Jesus and believe in your heart that God has raised Him from the dead, you will be saved. ¹⁰ For with the heart one believes unto righteousness, and with the mouth confession is made unto salvation."*

It's evident that *confession* is key in our journey of faith with God. So, don't short change what God desires to

GROOMING OUR INSIDES

do in your life by being irresponsible with the words that you allow to come out of our mouth (Proverbs 6:2). I want you to win in all areas of your life. Regardless of what you may be feeling or facing at this moment, I challenge you to start making positive confessions over your life today. There are a few pages throughout this book that contain "I AM Confessions" that you can speak over yourself. It's important that you make it a habit to inspect the words that are coming out of your mouth. No one's words have more power over your life than your own. Not only will we have to give an account for every word that comes out of our mouths (Matthew 12:34-37), but our very lives and future depends on it.

    I encourage you to also inspect the confessions of those that you have surrounding you. Monitor who is in your inner circle. Don't allow yourself to be surrounded by those who regularly speak doubt and unbelief. If you recognize that a friend or loved one around you is constantly speaking negativity or fear, pray about the relationship and consider voicing your concerns, but be aware that if no changes are made, it may be time to cut ties. Remember: your words frame your world. With God, you have a vision, a purpose and a calling that is too great and important for you to allow it to be truncated with negativity or words that contradict what God is speaking to you. You have a responsibility to yourself and more

It is important to confess over yourself WHO God says you are. Practice it now by looking in the mirror and confessing what God says about you. If you don't have a mirror, just use the mirror below, but visualize your reflection while you make these confessions over yourself.

- **I AM a daughter / son of the King of all Kings.** (Galatians 3:26-29).
- **I AM redeemed from my past, and my future is bright!** (Colossians 1:13-14, Proverbs 4:18).
- **I can do ALL things through Christ Who strengthens me.** (Philippians 4:13).
- **I am set apart for my Father's use; it is already done, in Jesus name!** (1 Peter 2:9, Deuteronomy 14:2).

Mirror, Mirror On the Wall

In whom does your confidence lie? Maybe your challenge isn't becoming obsessed with perfectly crafting your makeup or outfit to impress others. It could be halfway going broke to purchase the new Jordans or Louis Vuitton outfit that you know you can't afford, all in an effort to gain the esteem of your peers. Maybe it's blindly pursuing a degree that you feel will help better represent a certain social status, despite the fact that you know in your heart of hearts that God didn't tell you to seek after it or pursue that career. You ask yourself: "Should I be the polished, business professional today or the esteemed athlete?" "Is it straight diva-mode today or an intellectual vibe I want to give off today?" "Contemporary or urban?" Whatever it is, we have all been guilty at one point or another of falling into this same trap: morphing into whatever image we believe will be more acceptable to us.

Now let there be no confusion: there is nothing wrong with desiring to be fashionable and well put together. Your clothing and accessories do not define your identity, but they definitely do reveal a bit about who you are and about how you care for and value yourself. So, there is no problem with having a healthy self-image, good hygiene and wanting to look and feel nice. The problem only comes when we become obsessed and make our image, position or status an idol. When we allow this to happen, we eventually lose ourselves and who God created us to be.

We bear God's image for the purpose of giving Him glory. There is something that you were created to fulfill on this earth that only you can do the way that you do it. God gifted you with the ability to accomplish a specific assignment and to give Him glory through the unique gifts that He's entrusted to you while you are on earth. What are you doing with those gifts? Throughout your life, you may find yourself sharpening skills pertaining to your God given gifts, but those gifts will continue to remain dormant inside of you until you stir them up, practice and fine-tune them. Only you and God know the motivation

MIRROR, MIRROR ON THE WALL

behind your desires to accomplish what you do. We have to be honest with Him and ourselves and be willing to be humble enough to recognize when we need to just lay those desires on the altar and allow Him to burn away anything that is not of Him. It's important that we ask God to create a new heart in us so that our desires reflect His, and only mirror those things that are pure and honorable to God (Psalm 51:10).

As believers or Christ followers, the Bible should also govern our lives and dictate the parameters of our behavior and how we interact with others. It's a natural human tendency to question or seek validation of our worth or value. In fact, we live our lives constantly assessing the value of the people, places and things around us. Brand X paper towel is better than Brand Y. His net worth is five million while another young man's is just ten thousand. It can be a scary and unsettling living your life dependent on another man or woman's definition of your value. One reason is because man's opinion can literally change like the wind. One day someone may like you and the next they don't. What a relief it is to know that God loves us and always will. He already determined your value when He sent His most prized possession — His Son Jesus — to die for you, so that you could be saved from the eternal damnation that we deserved. Of course, salvation is a choice, but He deemed our spiritual and physical state to be important enough for Him to send His precious Son Jesus before we even made the decision to accept Him into our lives. He is a gentleman, and He will never force Himself on us. When we may be feeling unsure of ourselves, we can always trust in, stand on and depend on God's Word to find peace and closure on the fact that we are precious, loved and invaluable to our Creator.

God is all-powerful, and He knows the end from the beginning, but the decision to accept Christ and live for Him is ultimately ours. He thought us valuable, esteemed and precious enough to pay the ultimate price for us before we even decided to make the commitment to Him (John 3:16). Now, that's love! It's easy to love a person, when we know that we have the guarantee of that person's love being reciprocated, just as it is much easier to give when we know there is a chance of us receiving something back in return; but that is just the beauty of God's love, my dear friend.

THE WRONG MIRROR

A young woman who we'll call Sheila, endured a very troubled childhood. She suffered constant molestation and abuse at the hands of her father during her teenage years. For years, *Sheila suffered in silence*. She anxiously waited for her mother to intervene and stop the abuse, but her patience was fruitless. She became deeply depressed. Sadly, her mother had suffered the same abuse at the hands

MIRROR, MIRROR ON THE WALL

of her father, thereby leaving her paralyzed by fear and inactive in Sheila's life. Because it had remained hidden "in the family", it was never exposed and dealt with, so continued to loom and plague one generation to the next. Sheila's mom's heart ached for her daughter, but the shame of having not stood up for herself as a child or for her daughter wrecked her to the core, and the fear and condemnation ate her up inside. Like Sheila, she didn't know what to do and had lost all hope. At least that's the story that denial and fear held her hostage to accepting.

Growing up an only child, Sheila felt all alone. She had no one close to her that she could share about the adversities and inner turmoil she faced daily. She was self-conscious about her weight, her figure...her everything. So many nights, she peered into the lofty, antique mirror on her dresser, tears cascading down her face. She asked herself: 'What's wrong with me?' After all, it had to be something wrong with her, right? Why else would her father subject her to the abuse and trauma that he had? Why else would God allow it? If she really had worth and value, why else would her own mother remain mute when she knew the truth and saw the pain in her daughter's eyes? Because of her abuse, Sheila's self-image completely plummeted moving into her teenage years. She became obsessed with makeup, cosmetology and anything that could help her cover up who she really was. She was actually becoming

Cracked Mirrors

pretty skilled at it, but she hated the reflection that glared back at her in the mirror each night as she stripped off the heavy layers of foundation, blush and mascara.

Under each layer of makeup, she felt refuge and a little bit more comfortable in her skin. Perhaps it was because deep down, she felt it helped her to hide a reflection that she was truly ashamed of. Deep down, she felt she was ugly and inferior. Her self-image had been shattered, and her self-esteem was minuscule at best. Most of the time, her relationships, especially with those of the opposite sex, were in the context of friends with benefits. She flirted incessantly. Having relations with several of the guys at school literally just became a hobby of hers. Not really because she enjoyed giving herself to them in that way; she simply loved the attention that she received during each experience. In truth, they just told her what she wanted to hear so that they could get what they wanted. "Come here, beautiful…Girl, you know you fine." Deep down, she knew her male companions were only spitting game and, in the process, playing with her heart, soul and emotions, but that was okay with Sheila. With each pseudo escapade, she could pretend — at least for a few moments — to be the image of the woman that she envied so often, versus the one that she saw each night in the old cracked mirror at home before she cried herself to sleep. The irony was that even though she had been robbed or given up freely her

MIRROR, MIRROR ON THE WALL

virginity and purity, Sheila felt that she finally actually had some control of her life. That's what she thought.

There was a counselor at her school named Mrs. Washington who took special interest in Sheila. Mrs. Washington was a Christian and sensed that something wasn't quite right with Sheila personally or within her home environment. So, she pushed as far as Sheila would allow, to learn more, but each time, she felt like she kept hitting a wall. Sheila lashed out with anger and hurtful words, but Mrs. Washington was relentless. She knew she was called to love her back just as aggressively, so she did. After all, she knew the absent-minded stare in Sheila's eyes. She knew the anger all too well. After all, that had been her years ago before she'd given her life to Christ. He had not given up on her, and He totally turned her life around from the inside out.

Mrs. Washington felt led to love on Sheila just as hard. She rarely felt that she made any headway talking to Sheila, but each day, unbeknownst to her, she was gaining ground. Sheila could sense that she genuinely cared. "All the others would have gone missing a long time ago after what I said to her yesterday", Sheila said to herself, half-smirking even in her thoughts. Mrs. Washington dug until she found out about Sheila's interest in cosmetology and volleyball. She convinced her to try out for the team and to Sheila's surprise, she made it. Although it didn't fix the problems at home, Sheila found volleyball to be an extremely helpful outlet, and she was actually quite good. It was almost like she'd found new purpose for the moment. Months passed, and Mrs. Washington kept at it with Sheila: praying, loving, forgiving and encouraging.

On one special day before school when Mrs. Washington woke up and prayed, she could sense in her spirit that something was going to be different. Right after homeroom, Sheila was sent to the principal's office, who then sent her to the school counselor. She'd been a bit testy and disrespectful in class, but that's the way she had learned to manage her sanity by lashing out in order to protect her heart. She had to maintain some level of control in her mind for fear of having to face the reality that her world was really spiraling out of control and that she was helpless. The circumstances around her and her relationships only served to further validate her worthlessness. Mrs. Washington tried asking her about her behavior and thought that she had hit another wall, when it happened: Sheila broke. Shattered would probably more accurately describe what happened. Last night was no different than most at Sheila's house, but this time she'd had it. No more. She didn't want to end it all, but she was trying desperately to hold on to any glimmer of hope that something was going to change. She didn't consider herself to be a religious person, but she was searching for any prospect that God cared and that He

MIRROR, MIRROR ON THE WALL

would finally intervene.

So, when Mrs. Washington questioned her today, she couldn't hold back. She let out about everything: the abuse, her father, the boys... She shook uncontrollably as she poured out to Mrs. Washington about how depressed and lonely she was and about how frustrated she was with life itself. Inwardly, Sheila envied Mrs. Washington. She was beautiful, and she had the family, the job, she was funny and popular — everything Sheila ever wanted. Her life was perfect! She asked Mrs. Washington "How could a so-called loving God allow this to happen?" "Why did He create her so ugly and worthless?", she thought while she rambled on. She went on to ask Mrs. Washington why it was that she always seemed to be so happy and care free, while she was forced to live in so much pain? As much as Mrs. Washington's heart broke to hear about the pain that this young lady had endured, her heart also smiled a little inside. (You see, the Bible tells Christians to always be ready to give an answer for the hope that is inside (1 Peter 3:15), and she was ready. Mrs. Washington understood that God never promised us that we would not have any problems. In fact, it says, "in this world you will have tribulations, but be of good cheer, for I have overcome the world" (John 16:33). As believers, despite what's going on around us, we know where our hope and peace come from.)

Realizing she'd been crying for some time and that

her perfectly placed makeup must have been out of place, Sheila pulled out her compact mirror, dabbed her streaked mascara and responded: "I'm just so tired…and look, I'm a mess. Nothing will fix me or this messed up life of mine any — "Sheila", Mrs. Washington interrupted abruptly. "That's not true. I believe you're going to be okay. But, let's start here", she said, reaching over to grab and close Sheila's mirror compact. Sheila sat back, confused as Mrs. Washington slowly reached inside her purse and pulled out her faithful, worn Bible. "Sweetheart…you are absolutely beautiful. If only you were able to see it." Before Sheila even had time to interject, Mrs. Washington said, "You see the problem is…you're using the wrong mirror." This simple statement created the segue that Mrs. Washington needed to introduce Sheila to the infallible Mirror that is the Word, and its Author, her Creator, Who loved her like no other.

    Sheila didn't know any better at the time, but her problem was that she had allowed her circumstances, actions and opinions of others to define her value. The tragedies she suffered, especially at the hand of others, had no bearing on her value. In God's eyes, the value that He placed on her life had already been set prior to her having been faced with the adversities that she had in life. It was established when He sent down His Son, Jesus. For so long, her self-image had been so clouded by her past,

MIRROR, MIRROR ON THE WALL

failures and the hurt of others. Her vision was obstructed, and Mrs. Washington was endeavoring to point Sheila to look into the only Mirror that could really reveal just how beautiful, precious and gifted she really was.

DIRTY, BROKEN MIRRORS

Sin and the lack of a relationship with Christ can render us blind; it can rob us of vision and purpose. When we allow the enemy to creep into our lives and subject us to fear and condemnation or influence us to rebel against God, we set ourselves up to be manipulated by him and to accept a distorted, broken image of ourselves and our value. The Bible states that there is therefore no condemnation in our God (Romans 8:1). The Amplified version of this verse puts it this way: Therefore there is now no condemnation [no guilty verdict, no punishment] for those who are in Christ Jesus [who believe in Him as personal Lord and Savior].

I don't know what you are dealing with right now, but I want to encourage you to make this confession: "My past is over! It is finished, and I am forgiven, in Jesus' Name!" From God's perspective, there is no guilt or punishment from your past that He remembers once you ask Him for forgiveness (Micah 7:19. If you are reading this book, and you have not yet accepted Christ into your heart, I'm telling you that you are missing out on a loving relationship that is like no other that you will ever experience in life. Give

Cracked Mirrors

Jesus a try. I want to encourage you to accept Him into your heart right now. He loves you like no one else ever will or can, so before going any further in this book, if you'd like to have a relationship with Him now, please flip to page 169 and repeat the prayer shown.

To a degree, we are all cracked or slightly, dirty mirrors. While we were created by God and bear His image, after the fall of Adam in the Garden of Eden, we were separated from Him and His divine nature, and a sin nature was passed on to all mankind (Romans 5:12). If we go back and further expound on Genesis 1:26 using The Message translation, it says: God spoke: "Let us make human beings in our image, make them reflecting our *nature*..."

The Merriam-Webster dictionary defines **nature** a s *the inherent character or basic constitution of a person or thing; a creative and controlling force in the universe; an inner force (such as instinct, appetite, desire) or the sum of such forces in an individual*. We were created in God's image, but after the fall of man, we were separated from Him spiritually. God sent Jesus as a sacrifice so that we could be redeemed and reconciled to Him.

> *My old self has been crucified with Christ. It is no longer I who live, but Christ lives in me. So I live in this earthly body by trusting in the Son of God, who loved me and gave himself for me.* **—Galatians 2:20**

MIRROR, MIRROR ON THE WALL

When you make the decision to accept Christ, you allow Him to take residence in your hearts so that His nature can become your nature. Though we still live in an earthly body, we are able to pursue righteousness when we put our confidence in God and depend on Him for help. God's Word is true. In fact, it is the Truth. So it all boils down to whether or not we believe Him. Will you accept what God has to say about you or will you continue to debase yourself instead of accepting the feeble opinions of man? I plead with you to not accept the tarnished self-image that the devil is trying so hard to sell you. He is the father of lies (John 8:44), and there is no truth in him. Instead, turn to the Mirror of the Word.

God is not a man, so he does not lie. He is not human, so he does not change his mind. Has he ever spoken and failed to act? Has he ever promised and not carried it through? —**Numbers 23:19**

If you're tired of being lied to or disappointed or need someone you can trust, I have good news for you! There's no need to look any further, God cannot lie. In His Word we can and will find stability. His love for you will never change, and He will not change his mind about how valuable you are to Him no matter what. It's so comforting that we can rest in the fact that we do not serve a God who is flippant and indecisive, like man can be at times. It's sad how quickly people change not only their opinions but often even core beliefs. Well, when God speaks, He means what He says, and He always has our best interest at heart. With Him, we don't have to worry about getting taken advantage of or deceived. He is our Good Father. If we'll simply take the time to pray and meditate on His Word, we'll be delighted to find that our shame and insecurities will melt away.

When we view ourselves through the Mirror of His Word, there is no room for fear, doubt, shame, worry or anxiety because we can rest IN Him and none of those entities can abide in Him. Our Father loves us unconditionally despite our past failures or flaws. If we fall short, we have God's promise that He will forgive us (1 John 1:9). The ONLY eyes and opinions that really matter are those of your Creator. You are so loved and valuable to Him. Don't EVER allow any man or woman try to bring up your past for the purpose of demeaning you or discouraging you. You are a new creation in Christ Jesus (2 Corinthians 5:17). This means that God made you a new person IN Christ. Again, He doesn't remember our past failures like man does. The only good that your past should serve you now is to encourage others through your testimony of where God has brought you from.

MIRROR, MIRROR ON THE WALL

HELP, I'M A PEOPLE PLEASER!

Due to my own poor self-image growing up, I often subjected myself to unhealthy relationships because of the desire to be "approved of". I would override my conscious and the loving promptings of the Holy Spirit, and allow myself to be taken advantage of, all out of the desire of being approved. It's always been a part of my personality and desire to help and support others (and still is), and there's absolutely nothing wrong with that. The problem comes when it forces us to live an unbalanced life physically and spiritually. You risk being less effective, and it starts to bleed into other areas of your life. The Holy Spirit would prompt me, "He/she doesn't have your best interest at heart' or "Don't speak to them about your business..."; and I would foolishly ignore His warnings for the hope — the opportunity to once again be approved of by said individuals. Ridiculous, right?

I would work as unto the Lord, but I would go overboard at times because of this. My heart was right, but my life quickly became unbalanced because I did not prioritize properly. These bad habits became a way of life and quickly seeped into other areas of my life. In some cases, I would wait expectantly for the other person to tell me they were requesting too much or abusing the relationship because I knew they'd see it eventually. They weren't acting like it, but I just knew that somewhere, deep, deep down, they cared for my well-being and would stop demanding more, right? Wrong. I'll let you guess how those relationships ended and situations transpired. In truth, the Holy Spirit showed me that I really didn't like myself...or at least I didn't act like it. When I looked in the mirror, the reflection staring back at me was not that of what the mirror of God's Word would have shown me. I saw someone whose life was not worthy of setting proper boundaries. I saw someone whose time was not valuable enough to protect and guard as sacred enough to be kept from abuse or waste. I did not see myself as God saw me: a steward of the time that He had blessed me with to accomplish His will.

I somehow felt guilty of the thought of enjoying myself. I enjoyed my work professionally, but oftentimes when I should have been resting or enjoying life, I resisted it despite my own body screaming to me "STOP...You need to slow down!" As a result, on some occasions, I wrestled unnecessarily with some physical challenges that were further complicated by stress and anxiety. Though I am still growing in this area, it wasn't until I made a conscious decision to accept God's love for me that everything changed. I had to look into the Mirror and learn and embrace WHO I was and WHOSE I was. I am a daughter of the King of all Kings! Once I truly understood my value and that I was bought for a purpose, I had to receive His evaluation of me. If He deemed my life valuable and my

MIRROR, MIRROR ON THE WALL

calling significant, then I ought to value the temple that He gave me to house my spirit man here on earth.

Don't you realize that your body is the temple of the Holy Spirit who lives in you and was given to you by God? You do not belong to yourself, for God bought you with a high price. So, you must honor God with your body.
—1 Corinthians 6:19

In this passage, the Apostle Paul wasn't just simply expressing to the Corinthians their value in God's eyes. He was actually elaborating on that fact by explaining to them (and followers of Christ, at-large) that they should honor their bodies because of the high price that Christ paid on Calvary. This clearly shows that God expects us to honor our bodies and not abuse them. This is why we should do our best to not abuse our bodies with drugs, unhealthy lifestyles, or anything else. We risk abusing our bodies when we try to live up to the often-selfish expectations or desires of both others and ourselves.

When we exalt the opinion or approval of man over God's and allow ourselves to be controlled and manipulated, God isn't pleased. He desires for you to have life and to have it more abundantly (John 10:10), but the only way to maintain a balanced life and accomplish all that God has called us to, is to properly prioritize what is important and what is not. You have to take an honest evaluation and determine once and for all, what is worth allotting your time and focus on. Whether it is unhealthy habits, a job or even other people, ask God for wisdom with determining when things need to be preserved or eliminated out of your life, and He will help you.

God's not going to give you instructions to go accomplish an assignment and then send things your way that are constantly a stumbling block to you accomplishing them. We live in a fallen world, and the Bible tells us Satan is the god of this world (2 Corinthians 4:4). It's important to remember that test and trials will come your way, and God will ultimately use them to build patience and faith in your life. He doesn't waste anything — every test, failure, or flaw, can be used for His glory!

Always remember that nothing can replace you knowing the voice of God for yourself. He is not the author of confusion (1 Corinthians 14:33), and though sometimes we do have to ask God for understanding, He will not send you conflicting instructions. If you are having trouble understanding what the 'next steps' should be, take the time to ask God about it and spend time praying in the Holy Spirit. Seek the help of a mentor, if one is available. Just remember, He will not steer you wrong, and He will not abandon you. He desires to have an intimate relationship with you, so even if He blesses you with a mentor, it is

MIRROR, MIRROR ON THE WALL

not meant to replace your relationship with God or your sensitivity to the Holy Spirit. The words that that man or woman speaks into your life should only confirm what you feel the Lord is speaking to you.

ENTANGLED?

So many people pride themselves these days on being "woke" or intellectually elevated from the rest of society, but in actuality they live in a constant state of slavery and idolatry. Why do you say this, you may ask? Any habits or obligations that keep you from spending time in God's presence have become a form of bondage because they are interfering with your spiritual growth.

> *So put to death and deprive of power the evil longings of your earthly body [with its sensual, self-centered instincts] immorality, impurity, sinful passion, evil desire, and greed, which is [a kind of] idolatry [because it replaces your devotion to God].* —**Colossians 3:5 AMP**

Have you become so busy and entangled with the things of this world that you find yourself no longer having the time to spend time building and growing in your relationship with God? Just like any other relationship, you get out what you put in. God wants to use you (yes, YOU!) for His glory and to draw others to Him, but in order for this to happen, you have to be to discern His voice and obey it. You have to be willing to allow Him to fill you up with His love and compassion so that it radiates out to others. After all, you can't pour into others if you're an empty vessel, can you?

It is important to note that sitting in God's presence is no excuse to be lazy. So, if you are struggling with slothfulness or just seem to be paralyzed by fear in terms of walking in your purpose, ask God to help you with those areas as well. God has not given you a spirit of fear, but of power, of love and of a sound mind (2 Timothy 1:17), so get up and commit to doing all that God has called you to do. Trust Him and listen to His instructions; He will give you wisdom and He will never abandon you.

Be sure to take the time to sit before God's face daily to receive His peace, refreshing and instructions. If you have ever struggled with being stressed or over-worked as a result of taking on too many obligations and trying to save the world, then I'm sure you can relate to having come to the revelation after the fact that some task or request from the boss, friend or family member was simply just that… a request. It may have been a want improperly displayed as a need — another "Please! I've gotta have it right now!" When we allow ourselves to be controlled by every whim or desire of others, we not only set ourselves up to be abused, but we put ourselves in a position to form

MIRROR, MIRROR ON THE WALL

extremely bad habits that could eventually cause us to be sick, overwhelmed or completely forfeit God's plan and purpose for our lives due to stress or ill health. Furthermore, we may find ourselves trying to take on roles that only Jesus was equipped to handle anyway.

Oftentimes, we are disobedient to the instructions that God has given us because we are busy chasing a dollar or seeking the approval and acceptance of others. In many cases, the individuals that we are trying to please are simply self-absorbed and inconsiderate of the needs of others. They feel the world revolves around their desires and schedule regardless of the needs or responsibilities of others. God is not pleased with this type of behavior. However, sometimes the individuals are totally unaware of what other commitments and responsibilities we have, so it makes it even more imperative that we stand up for ourselves and set proper boundaries in our lives. It's our responsibility to open our mouths and respectfully set the boundaries that need to be set. This goes for work, family or church. We must respect God enough to properly take care of and protect our bodies and minds. After all, our bodies are the temple of the Holy Ghost, and we have the Holy Ghost living inside of us to help and comfort us and to give us wisdom. God wants our dependence to be totally on Him — not in a job, our family or friends' opinion of us and not in ourselves.

Cracked Mirrors

IS IT REAL?

I've been guilty of it myself in the past. It's easy to view the Bible as just another old storybook. For some scholars, the Bible is nothing but a history book with content that has somehow seemed to survive the test of time. But the Bible, our Mirror, is so much more than that!

For the **word of God is living and active and full of power** *[making it operative, energizing, and effective]. It is sharper than any two-edged sword, penetrating as far as the division of the soul and spirit [the completeness of a person], and of both joints and marrow [the deepest parts of our nature], exposing and judging the very thoughts and intentions of the heart.* — **Hebrews 4:12 AMP**

Just as God is still a **living, active, powerful God**, so is His Word. He loves you and wants to reveal things to you about yourself, other situations and sometimes others. If a stranger were to write you a deep, heartfelt letter or private message on social media sharing their admiration for you and belief in your abilities, gifts and talents, you may possibly, 1) look at them from a distance with raised eyebrows because it comes off as creepy, since they don't know you and haven't established that type of relationship or 2) smile at them (if they're in view), right before pushing the block button or 3) say thank you but then secretly

MIRROR, MIRROR ON THE WALL

wonder who they were and what qualifies them to even know what your gifts and talents were. Regardless of your natural response, one thing is for sure, the awkwardness of receiving the letter and the content of the letter exists primarily because there is no personal connection with the author. However, if your best friend or mentor gave you the exact same correspondence, your eyes may light up a bit or your heart may flutter. Why is that? It's because, in contrast to the previous correspondence, you have a personal connection to the author. You have history with one another. They are already acquainted with your gifts and flaws. They know the good, the bad and the ugly about you. The words resonate with you and somehow now appear to leap off the paper because you are familiar with the character of the one who wrote it and the authenticity of your relationship. Now you cherish each jot and tittle, and your eyes might linger slightly on every stroke of the handwriting because the previously lifeless piece of paper now emanates the value and worth that the author of the letter must place on you.

Well, it's the same thing with the Word of God. As you begin to spend time with God and learn more about the Author and His nature, that same book that previously only held the value of a text book now becomes a living, breathing testament of His love for you and all mankind. The more you take the time to reflect on the Word of

Cracked Mirrors

God and meditate on it regularly, the more the image and content lingers in your heart. You grow fonder of the Author because as He reveals to you more and more about His character, thoughts and viewpoints, you learn and trust His voice and His desires more easily. Like David in the book of Psalms, it should be our desire to know God on a deeper level.

> [15] I will meditate on Your precepts and [thoughtfully] regard Your ways [the path of life established by Your precepts]. [16] I will delight in Your statutes; I will not forget Your word. **—Psalm 119:15-16**

If you're not careful, self-doubt and fear can rob you of your dreams and purpose. As Christians, we are supposed to base our opinions and outlooks on the Mirror that is God's Word.

I have two siblings, and I am an aunt to two nieces and one nephew. My nieces are the younger of the bunch, and I'm so grateful that God graced me with the privilege of being involved in their lives from birth, through their infant and toddler years and beyond. Those two girls are some of the smartest, wittiest and most comical little humans that I know. There used to be an American comedy show named *Kids Say the Darnedest Things*. The premise of the show is that the host would ask a child around the age of

MIRROR, MIRROR ON THE WALL

3 to 8 a question, and the child would usually respond in a crafty, yet adorable fashion. Though they were much too young when the show aired, I've always said that they should have been on that show, but I digress…kind of.

One Sunday morning, I happened to be with them as they got ready for their children's church. They were at the age where you just knew that if they were in your care, you just got used to carrying around baby wipes to help keep their cute little faces free from crumbs, the occasional dribble and other debris. I used to talk to them and kid, "What's that? We've got to make sure those little pumpkins' faces are clean!" They'd laugh and giggle to themselves and sometimes run away from whomever was graced with that duty (oh the joys). Well, they got to the point where they used to stand still (as best they could) in front of you smiling proudly, as they waited for you to give their faces one final inspection, which was usually followed by a wash off with a warm cloth before loading up into the car for the service. It was a hilarious yet rewarding experience. On one occasion, one of them did something I'll never forget. As we prepared to go downstairs and load up the car to go to church, one of them, knowing they had crumbs — remnants from their morning snack on their face — hesitated beside the bedroom mirror but then turned abruptly towards me instead, looked up and said, "Auntie, is my face good [clean]?" I thought it was

Cracked Mirrors

too cute, and I went about my usual routine of wiping and double-checking her little face. It wasn't until later after God reminded me of the encounter, that I understood the full weight and value of that exchange. He said, "That's how I want you to be about My opinion of you." Did you catch that? The bedroom mirror beside my niece would have been the expected place for her to look to wipe off whatever was on her face. I mean, it's a mirror — that's what it's there for. Without hesitation though, my niece, who was only about 5 years old at the time, took my word about whether or not she was "okay" or presentable. She confidently trusted that I would tell her the truth about how she really looked more than what she perceived from her own reflection. Though it may seem insignificant, the magnitude of the importance of this lesson is great. What's even more spectacular is the fact that God wants us to possess the same childlike faith in Him and in His Word. He wants us to be so confident in our relationship with Him that we can trust His opinion about ourselves regardless of what the world or anyone in it thinks. Regardless of what the so-called experts in the fields of psychology fashion or any others say, we can trust God and that He will never write us off His list. He will always tell us the truth, and He will never steer us wrong.

What is THE Mirror showing you? What do you see when you spend time in His face and reflect on His Word?

MIRROR, MIRROR ON THE WALL

When we are quiet before God, He will speak to us. Whether you are feeling insecure about your complexion, weight, height, skill set, social status or whatever else, don't fret: you are fearfully and wonderfully made by your Creator (Psalm 139:14), and He is confident in your talents and abilities because He is the Giver of those gifts. Every good and perfect gift comes from Him (James 1:17). No matter what types of feelings of self-doubt and shame you may have faced or may be facing even now, rest in God's love for you and in your relationship with Christ.

At most nostalgic carnivals, there's a fairly popular attraction called a *carnival* or *fun house mirror*. These mirrors are constructed with a curved surface, so that instead of providing the viewer with a mirror image of themselves, the mirror instead provides a distorted image of the person standing in front of it. While fun house mirrors often produce many snickers and giggles at the carnival, it's not all fun and games when a distorted image manifest in our reality. God wants to crack some of the *false mirrors* that you've allowed to manifest in your life. You may have be obsessed with what family, co-workers or even false friends have had to say and what they think of you. You've been bewildered at your own self-image and value, and all the while, God is saying: "Daughter/son, one that I have fearfully and wonderfully made, come to me -- look to Me!" It doesn't matter. Nothing is too hard for our God. You can and will be WHOLE as you trust in Him totally as YOUR source. THE Source of what, you may ask? He is your Provider (Philippians 4:19), your Healer, your covering, your Peace…He is ALL that you need. And, He will perfect those areas in your life that concern you. Psalm 138:5 says, "The Lord will perfect that which concerns me; your mercy, O Lord, endures forever…"

God often uses our past or those parts about our physical or philosophical makeup that we may feel insecure about for the purpose of showcasing His glory and honor. His strength is made perfect in our weakness (2 Corinthians 12:9). Your testimony can help free someone of their past and restore their hope that God can and will use them in spite of their insecurities, hurts or past mistakes. When we are humble enough to admit to ourselves and others (if God leads) that we cannot do anything good on our own, we are setting the stage for God to use us for His glory. We've set the stage for the focus to be put on Him and not on our abilities.

It is always satisfying to sit back and reflect on the fact that our Creator actually took His time to intricately design every part of us: every bone, fiber, muscle and tendon… every organ. Our personality, gifts and talents were all perfectly assembled and assigned. Equally impressive is the fact that our Father God actually knows us by name. In John 10:3 it says, "The gatekeeper opens the gate for

MIRROR, MIRROR ON THE WALL

him, and the sheep recognize his voice and come to him. He calls his own sheep by name and leads them out." You may have noticed that God is often referred to as The Good Shepherd in the Bible. As a follower of Christ, God has called you by name. Just like a good shepherd cares for his sheep, God cares for His flock as well. He wants to lead your life. Though He is to be respected, it's not His desire to be known as the big, bad God in the sky. He desires to give you wisdom about the affairs of your life. He cares about each and every detail about you. In fact, our Father God is so pleased with your hair and its texture, that He took the time to number and catalog every strand of it (Luke 12:7), no matter how little or how much we have left (smile). You are beautiful and exquisitely designed!

I want to encourage you to never lose hope in the transforming power of God's love, especially when a man or woman (yourself included) turns to God. Nothing is too hard for Him. He is just, and He is not a respecter of persons. (Acts 10:34). That means that He doesn't show favoritism to a certain clique or class of individuals. Just as gazing at a reflection in a mirror can eventually influence one's self-image, if they don't understand their worth internally, reflecting on the Mirror —the Word of God — can impress upon one's heart and then eventually influence confidence and more importantly build one's faith.

It's important to God that we believe what He says

and thinks about us in comparison to what's going on in our world around us. When we are unsure about how to handle the affairs of our life, we know that God desires for us to go to Him for wisdom. He's not stingy with how much He gives either. The Bible says that He will freely give it to us (James 1:5)! This is exciting because it makes it plain to us that we don't serve a God who desires for us to be in the dark.

Reflecting on the Word of God and praying in the Holy Spirit is a great way for us to gain clarity, peace and direction about which path to follow as well as how we should respond to others. We don't have to live this life alone, wondering aimlessly. We don't have to be confused about what God's desires for us are. In fact, He doesn't deal with confusion (1 Corinthians 14:33). We need only trust Him and commit to patiently seeking His face. He will answer and give you peace on how to make important life decisions, but don't be afraid to open up and talk about the simple things in your life too. He cares about each and every detail!

Do you journal? If not, I'd like to encourage you to start. I've found that journaling sometimes helps in my time with God because it allows me to articulate what I'm feeling as well as write down what I believe He is saying to me. I want to encourage you as well to write down what you believe He's saying to you about your life as well.

MIRROR, MIRROR ON THE WALL

It also helps to track your growth and it will help you to create a log of what you may be praying and believing Him. If you don't have a journal, just grab a notebook or paper that you can easily store and archive If you don't have either, no worries: just right below.

Heart Reflections...

Go stand in front of a mirror (it doesn't matter if it's full length mirror or just a small hand-held one). Now look into it. Write down the first thoughts that come to your mind when you see your reflection.

_____
_____
_____
_____
_____
_____

Based on what you wrote above, does your interpretation of your reflection align with what God's Word says about you? In what ways today do you feel your viewpoint about yourself is a bit skewed?

_____
_____

Cracked Mirrors

_____
_____
_____

With God's help, I will work on:

_____
_____
_____
_____
_____

Gems to Reflect On...

All Scripture is inspired by God and is useful to teach us what is true and to make us realize what is wrong in our lives. It corrects us when we are wrong and teaches us to do what is right. God uses it to prepare and equip his people to do every good work. **—1 Timothy 3:16-17**

Whatever is good and perfect is a gift coming down to us from God our Father, who created all the lights in the heavens. He never changes or casts a shifting shadow. **—James 1:17**

For I know the plans I have for you," says the Lord. "They

MIRROR, MIRROR ON THE WALL

are plans for good and not for disaster, to give you a future and a hope. **—Jeremiah 29:11**

If after reflecting on the previous chapter, you feel that your self-image may just be a bit skewed, will you join me by praying the prayer below? Feel free to make it your own.

PRAYER TO THE FATHER

Father God, I know that you love me. I recognize that somewhere along the way, I've allowed the world to dictate my value and self-image. Somewhere along the way, my image of myself has been skewed. Lord, help me to view myself through the Mirror of Your Word and in the light that Your love and sacrifice of Your Son Jesus has clearly demonstrated. I confess today that I am your son / daughter, and I am fearfully and wonderfully made by you. My gifts, talents and abilities are second to none because they are one of a kind. I will trust in you to reveal to me your purpose for my life. I will not be discouraged by emotions, the opinions of others or my present circumstances, because my confidence is in you and not in my own intellect, emotions or the opinions of others. I believe that the work that you started in me, will be completed and perfected until the day of Christ Jesus (Philippians 1:6).

Thank you Father for loving me. I call it all done, in Jesus' mighty Name. Amen!

Letting God Clean Our Mirror

REFLECTING ON THE PAST

To describe Susan's past and upbringing as *unsettling* would be quite the understatement. During her early teenage years, her mom did the best she could, but struggled with her own past – dealing with both the assumed murder of a sister at a young age and an addiction to marijuana and alcohol. She also sold drugs, so was simply oblivious to Susan's adolescent trauma. Susan's father was around but to say he was *in the home* would have been a stretch. Susan's mom and dad fought constantly, especially about his running the streets with other women; and he often came home drunk or high. Though they sometimes successfully kept up appearances to outsiders as a normal family, inside, the home environment was tumultuous. Yes, during Christmas, they always had the best in the neighborhood: the most flamboyant Christmas lights and gifts. They got bikes, keyboards, nice radio systems – whatever they wanted. But without much direction in the home, Susan was left feeling empty, vulnerable, naive and susceptible to more than she'd ever imagined.

Even in her innocence, Susan's self-esteem had already begun to slowly plummet because of favoritism, racial undertones and self-hate within her own family. You see, Susan's complexion was as dark as the night, while her sister and grandmother were more fair-skinned with wavy hair to boot. Susan's grandmother was very attractive, educated, held several degrees and served as an associate pastor at the neighborhood church where she grew up. Susan's sister preferred not to be associated with her, so young Susan just floated around whoever was open to her being there. The irony was that while Susan sat day-after-day, vulnerable to the cruel influences of her environment, her grandmother would make a special effort to fly her sister all over and expose her to the world. She invested, time, energy and money into her while Susan suffered in silence, not even properly learning to communicate or

LETTING GOD CLEAN OUR MIRROR

to interact socially. She had no memories of even being helped with her homework.

Unfortunately, the lack of supervision in the home led Susan to fall victim to abuse, rape and much more than she ever could have imagined during her teenage years. Around her thirteenth birthday, Susan's family moved to a neighborhood with more of an imperious reputation. It was here that she met a girl that we'll call Snooks. Snooks was fast and street-wise while in contrast, up until this point, Susan had always been fairly quiet and to herself, but extremely naive. Unfortunately, this naiveness was a magnet for the wrong company. Snooks, who was a few years older than Susan, had taken some interest in her, but not for the reason Susan thought. On one occasion, unbeknownst to Susan, Snooks had passed her phone number to the guys in her crew, and they began to call her. These guys were extremely promiscuous, and as you've probably imagined, sexually active. The boys were in their mid-teens and had been with strippers, in gangs – you name it, but Susan was clueless to who she was surrounding herself with.

Deep down, all she really wanted was for someone to give her attention and to love her. One of the guys in this group took a special liking to Susan because he could sense from a mile away her level of naiveness and innocence. For a little while, he satisfied Susan's immediate need of being accepted. Unfortunately, it was with this very same individual that Susan experienced the first of 3 incidents of rape. "Get off me! STOP! Get away from me! You didn't ask my permission!" were all expressions that were frozen in time within the confines of Susan's heart and soul, but somehow, they would not funnel down to her mouth to say them. Each time, she went into a state of shock that prevented her from defending herself, speaking or stopping the perpetrator in any way.

As a result, Susan was vulnerable to more incidents of abuse. Even though her countenance revealed she was angry, she became an easy target for others. She soon started acting out at school and having altercations with her teachers, because it was difficult to articulate what was really happening to her inside. Not long after this, Susan found out she was pregnant. Unfortunately, she was still so young and unaware of her body makeup and biology. She didn't understand all the symptoms that she was experiencing. When her mom found out about the pregnancy, she was saddened, in shock and upset. Even though she was doped up half the time herself, it didn't stop her mind from wondering "Just how did my daughter end up in this predicament anyway?". After all, she was barely a teenager. Susan was not capable of caring for a child on her own - she was practically still a child herself. But instead of even attempting to explain the dynamics of the situation, Susan's mom took it upon herself to make

LETTING GOD CLEAN OUR MIRROR

that decision for her daughter. In all honesty, Susan had not even heard of the word abortion prior to the day her mother drove her to the clinic. This ignorance was only compounded by the complexities of the emotional and physical trauma that would soon follow thereafter.

Susan was haunted by memories of her abortion throughout most of her teenage years: the coldness of the room where her unborn child was unjustly taken away from her at such a young age, the eerie feeling of deadness in her womb that she somehow shared with all the other women that lay there in that room post-abortion.

Though she endured quite a few more challenges after her abortion, it was definitely by God's grace and love that Susan was later exposed to the Gospel through a co-worker years later. She was a babe in Christ and her relationship with God was a process in itself, but Susan immediately sensed God's love and His presence and experienced true deliverance from her past. She had to make a decision for herself to release and forgive her abusers, and even her mom and dad in order to move forward.

To this day, nobody can convince Susan that God isn't real and that His promises aren't true because she has seen first-hand how He redeemed her and set her free. Her self-image is no longer clouded with a shadow of doubt and fear. He alone was responsible for restoring her sanity and peace of mind. He alone was responsible for repositioning her in her purpose and His plan for her life despite the residue of her past. He totally revolutionized Susan's life for His honor and glory, and He can do the same in your life! He is no respecter of persons (Romans 2:11)!

DEALING WITH HURT & PAIN

Dealing with hurt and pain isn't always easy. Sometimes, when we're insecure or just hurt from our past, it's as if we are viewing everything through a distorted glass or dirty mirror. Hurt or abuse from the past makes it difficult to understand or process things accurately in our lives. You may be dealing with or have dealt with the heartbreak of a divorce, separation, death or even the trauma of domestic violence or abuse and are finding it difficult to navigate it all. Regardless of where you may find yourself today, God instructs us to not give place to the enemy in our lives by allowing anger or fear to control us. Unforgiveness and resentment can leave an open door for the devil to swoop in and wreak havoc in your life. We can't allow bitterness to fester in our hearts because it is destructive (Ephesians 4:26-27).

God is Love, so it's important to Him that we are making a conscious effort to walk in love with those around us. When someone hurts us or offends us, we must learn how to forgive and release them with the same fortitude that we used to somehow muster up to forget our own. In

LETTING GOD CLEAN OUR MIRROR

other words: God forgave us of our sins and shortcomings no matter how great or small we viewed them at the time, and in His eyes, there is no totem pole for sin. He is a holy God and to Him, sin is just sin. More importantly, every time that we hold bitterness and unforgiveness in our hearts, it's like someone putting mud or other debris on the mirror of our hearts. God wants to propel us into our purpose, but we can't walk the path He's set because our vision is clouded.

For a portion of my life, I battled with feelings of insecurity and rejection. Part of the insecurity was due to misconceptions during my upbringing that led to feelings of low self-worth. Some were perpetuated by others who may have felt that they were superior to me, maybe aesthetically, intellectually or athletically – who knows? As a result, some showed disdain, laughed or ridiculed me because I and others were "different". The ironic thing is that God later showed me that the very ones who gloated over their false perception of "self-value" were actually perpetuating indications that they themselves had low self-esteem. In their eyes, their value was increased by how low they could make others feel about themselves or by what clique they were associated with. This happens when one's value is erroneously placed in him/herself, associations or things instead of in Christ. God desires for us to have human companionship, but He never desired for us to allow the opinions of other humans to negate His will. He also never intended for us to allow our loyalty to others to cause us to reject and disobey His promptings and instructions for our lives.

CLARIFIED VISION

As you grow more and more in the things of God, you will find that your vision of Christ is clarified. When I was in junior high, I remember taking one of my annual trips to the optometrist. My eyes had been giving me a little issue but upon further evaluation, it was determined that I was desperately in need of glasses to help with distance. Though I wasn't particularly thrilled with the new addition to my wardrobe, one of the first things I noticed once I put on the new glasses was how incredibly clear everything was. No, I wasn't blind before (haha), but the detail that I was now privy to was nothing short of amazing. Things that I had simply grown accustomed to being blurry or barely visible, I could finally see. I mean I literally saw the world with a new set of eyes! It's one thing to have your sight restored to see what you haven't been able to in a while; it's another thing to have your vision clarified to a state that you never even knew existed.

So it is in our relationship with our Heavenly Father! When we begin to view things in light of the Word of God, it's as if we're a 100-20, near-sighted teenager who's never seen the world in true living color the way it's

LETTING GOD CLEAN OUR MIRROR

supposed to be seen later being exposed to a brand new world! When we turn our eyes away from God, and we don't meditate on the Word of God and instead lean on our own understanding, the mirror becomes cloudy and our reflection becomes distorted. This distorted reflection almost always yields to a fractured self-image or a lack of confidence. When you know who you are in Christ, you can be walking down the street with 2 pennies in your pocket, but have all the peace and confidence then anyone else around you because of your relationship with Christ. You know that He's got you, that He's walking with you and that the circumstances you're facing are only temporary.

When we begin to gain an accurate picture of just how God's grace has saved and redeemed us, we begin to understand just how valued and loved we are. You may be asking, "How do I overcome the insecurities of my past?", "How do I move past the roadblocks I'm currently facing in my life?" Well, that's the thing, friend: if we could truly do it on our own, then we wouldn't be in need of a Savior, a Helper and a Redeemer, would we? Seek God's help, and He will heal you from the hurt of from your past or past failures, and give you wisdom and discernment on how to move forward. He heals the broken-hearted and He binds up their wounds (Psalm 147:3). It doesn't matter what adversities you face in life and who or what tries to present itself/himself/herself against you, they CANNOT and WILL

Cracked Mirrors

NOT prevail with God on your side…period! God desires for you to live a prosperous life, but it all lies on the other side of your obedience and forgiveness. The longer it takes us to release our past, the longer it may take for us to truly step into our calling.

There is bondage in unforgiveness. You have to make a decision that you are not satisfied with continuing to live a life enslaved to fear, regret or shame. Refuse to live a life imprisoned by bitterness, hurt and unforgiveness. In order to truly be healed and to step into God's calling for your life, you must spend time in His presence to get divine instructions from Him. We have to gaze intently into the Mirror of His God's Word and meditate on what He says about us and the circumstances that we face in life in order to carry out the vision that God has given us.

It is still absolutely amazing to me how God can give you such a peace even when you're dealing with a challenging situation or what you may feel at the time may be the most difficult period of your life. In Isaiah 26:3, the Bible says, "You will keep in perfect peace all who trust in you all whose thoughts are fixed on you!" Now, if we go back and re-read the verse in the Amplified translation, it further elaborates that God will give this man or woman perfect peace because he commits himself to God, leans on Him, and hopes confidently in God. It would appear that our dependence on God is somewhat of a prerequisite for

LETTING GOD CLEAN OUR MIRROR

enjoying this "perfect" peace. It comes through meditating and keeping your mind on God. It comes through faith and by trusting in Him.

2 Corinthians 5:17 says, "Therefore, if anyone is in Christ, he is a new creation; old things have passed away; behold, all things have become new". In short, that lets us know that once we give our lives to Christ, from that point on, our identities, our DNA, is in Christ and everything He is, and this includes His character and attributes. God cares so much for you. It doesn't matter how you may be feeling right now about your abilities. You matter and you ARE enough. Trust that the Creator knows better the purpose of His creation than it does. We must seek God's approval more than man's. Those who are obsessed with the thoughts and approval of man often allow themselves to be manipulated and abused by others. They live in a constant state of fear, especially the fear of rejection. So, it's important to note that the Bible tells us that perfect love drives out fear (see 1 John 4:18 AMP).

When we are walking in fear, it is impossible for us to step out and walk in faith. No matter your past or background, I want to encourage you to allow God to heal you. Even if you've slipped up, God's grace is sufficient.

[10] He does not punish us for all our sins; he does not deal harshly with us, as we deserve. [11] For his unfailing love

Cracked Mirrors

toward those who fear him is as great as the height of the heavens above the earth. ¹² He has removed our sins as far from us as the east is from the west. **—Psalm 103:10-12**

Ultimately, you have to allow God to deal with anyone who may have hurt you. It is not our responsibility to seek revenge on anyone who has hurt or offended us. Bring God all of your fears, worries, hurts and flaws and ask Him to remove them from you; allow Him to create a whole new heart inside of you (Psalm 51:10). When you are walking in unforgiveness, it penetrates every area of your life like a slow, seeping venom through the veins. It affects your vision and discernment of situations, and it's impossible for you to be able to see clearly until the venom is extracted from your heart. So, push through those feelings of anger, bitterness, betrayal, or resentment for your own preservation and victory. There is so much more on the other side of your hurt and pain. God wants to go before you and make the crooked places straight. He wants to heal you so that He can take you to the other side!

Again, it is so important for you to ask God for help. He told us in His Word, "If you need wisdom, ask our generous God, and he will give it to you. He will not rebuke you for asking" (James 1:5). He desires to help you because He wants you to win and be successful in life. He will show you how to deal with certain people and

LETTING GOD CLEAN OUR MIRROR

situations and literally give you the right words to say.

When you realize that you too were graced in some area to be where you are today, it will become challenging to look down at the shortcomings and failures of others when you realize that you too were graced in some area to be where you are today. Oh, how I thank God for His grace! His mercies are indeed NEW every morning and are everlasting (Lamentations 3:23).

What setbacks in your life have you allowed to distract you and get you off course? The process of living a purpose-filled life is not a sprint; it's a marathon. So, don't be discouraged by temporary failures. We are all working out our salvation (Philippians 1:12), but we just have to learn to commit to trusting God through the process. We have to be dependent on God and put more confidence in Him than we do in any of our past failures, flaws or idiosyncrasies. We have to put more confidence in God than we do in the opinions or thoughts of others and even of ourselves. As you begin to spend more time with your Father, you'll find that His voice gets more and more familiar. Just like a relative or good friend, if you spend time with a person and get to know them, their likes and dislikes and their passions, you will become more confident and familiar with the character of that individual. Jesus tells the disciples in John 10:27 that His sheep listen and know His voice. He says, "I know them, and they follow me." Don't give up. Our relationship with God should be an organic one. The more we grow in Him, the more confident we are in stepping out in faith and committing wholeheartedly to Him.

If you feel that you are struggling with severe depression, from soul ties that stem from a broken relationship (friendship or otherwise), rejection or simply having difficulty moving forward, I encourage you firstly to go sit at the feet of Jesus. That means to set aside time to get on your knees and vent to Him. Tell Him what you're struggling with; tell Him your frustrations and fears. You can be honest with Him without being concerned about your confidentiality being violated. Ask Him for His help and for Him to show you anything that you need to be aware of that may have become a roadblock in your life. Sometimes, it's just asking for forgiveness for holding offense in our hearts against someone else. It's even possible to hold offense in our own hearts against ourselves because of regret from the past. I'm begging you not to forget that God is there to help. Secondly, it is always helpful to seek wise counsel (Proverbs 11:14). Set up an appointment with your pastor. If one is not available, please seek out advice from a Christian counselor or a trusted mentor, who is qualified by experience to assist you. God wants you free from any weight of the past, but we have to take the first step. If we're not careful, hurt, setbacks or mistakes from our past can put a crack in the mirror of our soul's reflection. They can

LETTING GOD CLEAN OUR MIRROR

become a trigger for self-doubt, which inevitably leads to low self-esteem. Low self-esteem can invite procrastination because when we doubt our self-worth, we can begin to second-guess the ideas, wisdom and instructions we receive from God. Before we know it, we lack the confidence to fulfill and obey the call that God has placed on our lives because we are paralyzed by fear. It's so important that you press past the traps of self-doubt.

In the past, I have been labeled as a "workaholic", an over achiever, super-sensitive, thoughtful, creative, you name it. Sometimes the world can place labels on what they don't understand or envy, vainly attempting to characterize what they are ill-equipped to accept. Don't ever be afraid or ashamed to be all of who God created you to be and don't buy into the lies that the enemy tries to sell you, telling you that you aren't enough. You are beautiful, unique and one-of-a-kind. Again, there's no point of settling; you do this every time you try to fit into the molds of what society characterizes as normal, hip or acceptable because you are incredibly unique and love by God. Of course, you don't go out of your way trying to be eccentric or abnormal just to get attention — that's just as bad — because this behavior simply exposes the fact that you are uncomfortable with who you are. It implies that your value and worth can be determined based on society's opinions of you or your desire to be accepted. We are most fulfilled in life when we are pursuing the unique plans that God has drafted for us. This is because we are made whole in Christ.

So you also are complete through your union with Christ, who is the head over every ruler and authority.
—Colossians 2:10

And I am certain that God, who began the good work within you, will continue his work until it is finally finished on the day when Christ Jesus returns. **—Philippians 1:6**

Your pain can be transformed into your passion when you allow God to use your past and testimony to help others that are struggling with similar issues to the ones that He has already brought you through. Allow Him to use your past hurts and pains for His glory. Nothing is wasted with God, every hurt, pain, failure that you've encountered in life, can be recycled for His purpose. Not only can your testimony serve as a reminder to the goodness of God and how He has brought you through before, but it can also eventually bring comfort and deliverance to someone else. The mission is always greater than just us. He loves you, and He wants to use you to help others and reflect His love to them.

LETTING GOD CLEAN OUR MIRROR

Heart Reflections

Are there any issues from your past that have stopped you from moving forward? Is there anyone that you need to forgive or release in order to move forward? If so, right down those areas of concern and then take them to your Heavenly Father.

_____
_____
_____
_____
_____
_____
_____
_____
_____

After that, make this declaration once and for all:
I will not be bitter or resentful to those who have hurt me in the past. I forgive those who have hurt me, and I forgive myself. I will move forward into the purpose and plan that God has called me to using the gifts, talents and abilities that He has entrusted me with. God has healed me, restored me and made me whole. I am a new woman / man. I am more than a conqueror (Romans 8:37)!

Reflections of:

MS. OLGA MESHOE (soon to be "Washington"): *36 year old, all-round hard-working young woman who is passionate about young people and Africa's development for the glory of God*

When you reflect on your image in the mirror, who do you see?
A young woman upon whom God's hand rest. I have experienced many mountain highs and valley lows and continue to be amazed at God's faithfulness in and through them. I know that I am yet to reach my full potential and am humbled, excited and 'nervous' about what the future holds.

Summarize yourself prior to accepting Christ using 3 words:
Because I have been saved since I was 7, so I don't really recall how I saw myself prior to accepting Christ.

How does the viewpoint of the reflection that you see now differ from the person you were before your relationship with Christ? What's changed?
N/A

What was one of the most influential events in your life that influenced your

perspective now or your relationship with Christ, as a whole?

I got divorced after 2.5 years of marriage. As a pastor's kid and eldest child of parents of prominence within the South African church and community, there was a lot of judgment and commentary: people left our church and I carried a lot of condemnation (there is also a stigma around divorced people, especially woman, in the church). I experienced God's tangible, unmerited love, grace, forgiveness and mercy. I am now in a season where I am experiencing His joy and redemption. In summary, the event caused me to practically experience aspects of God's character that I only previously knew theoretically.

**How did God change your image?
Share in three words:**

Beautiful • Redeemed • Favored

It is important to confess over yourself WHO God says you are. Practice it now by looking in the mirror and confessing what God says about you. If you don't have a mirror, just use the mirror below, but visualize your reflection while you make these confessions over yourself.

- **I AM not fearful because God has not given me a spirit of fear.** (2 Timothy 1:7).
- **God gives me a peace that passes all understanding; He guards and protects my heart and mind.** (John 14:27)
- **No weapon formed against me prospers and EVERY tongue that comes against me in judgment is condemned in Jesus' mighty name!** (Isaiah 54:17)

Our God of Peace

As I alluded to earlier, for a portion of my life, I dealt with anxiety. Anxiety over work-related tasks, over concerns about my life and the future, about the thoughts and opinions of others…about a lot. It was so extreme on occasion that I started grinding my feet into the soles of my shoes to get some release from my anxiety. Now, before we go any further — I know this may sound weird or unheard of to some, but bear with me. Oftentimes, we turn to unhealthy habits or behaviors to get temporary relief from pain that we may be facing. For some, it may be drinking, smoking, having sex outside of marriage, gambling, doing drugs…the list goes on. We make those temporary outlets a god by exalting them over God and the help that only He can provide. I believe that I am no greater than Christ, and if He made Himself of no reputation for us, then who am I to not do the same, if it gives Him glory? Being vulnerable about our weaknesses not only allows us to see how desperately we are in need God's redemptive power, but it also allows us to point others to Christ because His strength is made perfect in our weakness (2 Corinthians 12:9-10). Now back to the story. This all occurred during a season in my life where I found myself in the aftermath of dysfunctional relationships / friendships. The Holy Spirit is a Teacher (John 14:26) and reflecting back years later, He showed me times where my actions contributed in the decline of a relationship. He showed me where I handled situations in a manner that He was pleased, and He showed me where there was room for improvement. As a matter of fact, on some occassions, I also recalled that when there was confrontation, I could help to deescalate the situation by showing no emotion. Allowing any emotion to show could trigger more anger or discontentment from others. (Being completely honest with you, avoiding or eliminating confrontation was a bad practice I'd adopted way before these incidents occurred. As a result, this was the state of my every day life years later.) Things were to the point where I knew that crying or complaining would be futile. I could always just vent or cry later. So, what was my temporary solution? I would just channel whatever stress, fear and anger down to my

OUR GOD OF PEACE

feet where it would go unnoticed. I'd literally grind my feet at the soles until I found some type of temporary relief. In hindsight, it was kind of like the behavior alone served as a giant stress ball, but it is not God's desire for us to live in a constant state of stress and worry. The shoes in my shoe closet at the time bared the burden of this toxic behavior. The idiom *before you judge a man, walk a mile in his shoes* is typically used as an admonition to practice empathy in our everyday lives, but it gained an all new meaning in that moment. One would have found it shocking to examine never mind walk in my shoes; I held it in well.

Before I knew it, I was carrying this over to other areas of my life but instead of vocalizing hurt and offense, I would just push it down. In truth, this behavior had taken root in my life much earlier on in life. My emotions didn't even have time to connect with my reality for fear of facing my imperfections and tarnishing the grimy, self-righteous image staring back at me. Because I also struggled with perfectionism and pleasing others, the impact of failure seemed to hit me harder than most. So, instead of facing the problem, I'd delay the inevitable. "I'll deal with it later", I told myself. "There's time", I'd say. The Word of God — our Mirror – tells us about the dangers of bitterness and holding hurt and unforgiveness in our hearts:

[14] *Work at living in peace with everyone, and work at*

Cracked Mirrors

living a holy life, for those who are not holy will not see the Lord. ¹⁵ Look after each other so that none of you fails to receive the grace of God. Watch out that no poisonous root of bitterness grows up to trouble you, corrupting many. **—Hebrews 12:14-15**

How many times have we fought and suffered in a silent war of unforgiveness? We talked earlier about the effects of holding hurt in, but bitterness can also rob you of your joy, your peace and even your relationship with God. It could be due to fear of being deceived or hurt again or fear of moving forward. It is important to know that the Word of God tells us that fear has torment (1 John 4:18). Our insides are in turmoil and our lives a wreck, but we mask it — we cover it up, instead of running to the Father and venting to Him. Jesus tells us, "Come to Me, all who are weary and heavy laden, and I will give you rest" (Matthew 11:28). So many times, we exalt our problems and fears over the Creator of the universe. When we take on problems and the cares of this world, we take on weights that we were never equipped to handle in the first place.

Anxiety and worry take residence in our lives and hearts when we make the decision — whether consciously or unconsciously — to rely on our own understanding instead of in our Father God. Instead of looking into the Mirror and seeking God's help, we try to self-diagnose and medicate

OUR GOD OF PEACE

the problem. This usually produces unfavorable results. The Bible instructs us to lean not on your own understanding (Proverbs 3:5-6) for a reason. God wants us to run to Him and depend on Him. Besides, He already knew about the challenges you were going to face before they came your way. When I was going through my situation, I started to rely on my intellect to aid in "figuring things out". There is some scientific proof that when dealing with a distressing event, we are psychologically programmed to try to cope with the trauma incidents. As a result, I was clueless to the fact that certain interactions in relationships throughout my life had affected me on a much deeper level emotionally than I could have ever imagined. I tried to be the hero like I was invincible, skating along trying to be the rock for everyone else, but I was living a lie.

My constant ritual of internalizing my feelings soon turned to numbness; and the numbness wouldn't allow me to feel the pain or shame because facing it meant reckoning with the truth of my present reality, my failures and becoming totally unnerved at the seams of my vulnerable state. The anxiety that took over during that time resurfaced years later and led to the same behaviors, desolation of many pairs of shoes and other objects. When we don't run to God during stressful situations but instead try to handle things ourselves, we resort to fruitless attempts at seeking peace. Regardless of the vice, when we try to take things into our own hands, we're telling God that we don't trust Him unconditionally. We're communicating to Him that we don't think He is mighty and capable enough to handle our personal situation. We're making the problem an idol because we are exalting it over our Father God. Ultimately, we end up unfulfilled because during the storms of life, we are trying to seek relief and peace through sources that are ill equipped to give it.

It took me a while to realize it, but I came to see that I had adopted a very unhealthy mental outlook. The Holy Spirit revealed it to me one day very clearly. God desires for us to live in a constant state of inner peace. I don't care if you've resorted to cutting, taking drugs, or having sex to deal with the rejection, hurt, shame or failures from your past or present, I'm here to tell you that Jesus loves you, and He wants you healed and whole! Do not accept the lies of the enemy. He is a liar and a defeated foe! You will make it, you will smile again and you will accomplish great things for the Kingdom of God as you put your trust in God and totally rely on Him. He desires to destroy any negative self-image that we may hold in our hearts, and He wants to disclose the motives of our hearts (2 Corinthians 4:5 AMP). Sometimes, we may even be oblivious to what is going on within our own psyche and heart, but God is omniscient; He knows all. The Bible says that the spirit of a man knows the things of a man (1 Corinthians 2:11).

OUR GOD OF PEACE

The part of you that is your spirit is aware of things that your mind may not even be aware of, but we have to be willing to go to God and meditate on what His Word says about what we are facing and then allow Him to speak to us through the Holy Spirit. The word introspection is often used when one is endeavoring to describe some deep state of evaluating their inner self. However, as bearers of God's image, we have the privilege of true and authentic introspection, when we view our reflection in THE Mirror of God's Word.

In my situation, on the outside, I guess I looked okay. If the mirror represented the reflection of what others could see, you would say that I was holding all the pieces together in an effort to reflect that poised demeanor they'd grown so accustomed to. However, beneath the surface, there were emotional, hairline fractures that were only temporarily masking the severe internal trauma that lay just beneath the surface. I don't think there's room in this book to even begin to explain all that I went through, but it got to the point where I literally no longer cared whether I lived or died because of the embarrassment and regret of having failed were overwhelming to me at the time, and these feelings were amplified due to the fact that I was such an extremely private person. I saw no way out and thought that I would lose my mind at times, but God! In 2 Timothy 1:7, it says, "For God has not given us a spirit of fear, but of power and of love and of a **sound mind**". I think we often underestimate the power and significance of the latter part of that verse. A sound mind: what does that mean? The Amplified version of the same verse describes it as "...a calm, well-balanced mind..." Well-balanced is defined in the Merriam-Webster dictionary as "nicely or evenly balanced, arranged, or regulated; emotionally or psychologically untroubled." **Untroubled.** Yes, God's primary reason for sending His Son Jesus was to save us, His beloved, from eternal spiritual death in hell and to give us a way out. However, He wasn't just concerned about our spiritual state. He's our Father, and like any good father, He desires for us to live and exist in wholeness: healed and whole physically, emotionally, psychologically and redeemed spiritually. In contrast, it's our enemy's (Satan) desire to totally destroy our existence (John 10:10) with condemnation, fear and ultimately death.

Maybe you're feeling like, "Tiara, you just don't understand. I've blown it! There's no turning back because I've messed up too bad. God can't forgive me and love me…completely." Maybe you're thinking: "You don't know what I've done. There's no way He could love me. I'm too broken and ashamed. I let it go too far." The Bible says that Satan is the accuser of the brethren (Revelation 12:10). He wants to beat you up with shame by throwing in your face the failures and mistakes from your past. He wants

OUR GOD OF PEACE

you paralyzed and rendered helpless to move forward into God's purpose for your life. Well, I'm here to encourage you brother/sister: if you are a believer, then the God that is in you is greater than any flaw or mistake from your past. There is nothing that can separate you from God's love and forgiveness if you will just come to Him. Run to Him! So what if you don't have confidence in yourself right now? That's totally fine. You're right where God wants you: totally dependent on Him.

Don't forfeit your divine destiny and calling by listening to the devil. I repeat: he is "a defeated foe" (Hebrews 2:14-15). This is one of the rare times where it's okay to place all your eggs in one basket. Place ALL your confidence in God. We can trust Him and rest confidently in Him no matter the situation because He cares for us unconditionally, and He's already proven it by giving us His most prized possession: His Son Jesus Christ.

DEPRESSION

I am not a clinical psychologist nor do I claim to be, but I don't want to totally neglect a very real issue that many people, including followers of Christ, have been challenged with; and that's the issue of depression. It's something that we have all probably dealt with in the mix of emotional ups and downs and disappointments. However, we have to be careful that we don't allow our emotions to be affected

Cracked Mirrors

by demonic influence that leads to deep depression.

People may be more susceptible to depression for a variety of reasons. As always, we can reflect in the Mirror to see an example of this. Many times when we read the Bible, we subconsciously forget that the characters we read about were real people who dealt with real emotions and difficulties on occasion. In fact, all throughout the Bible, we see many examples of many men and women who also suffered from bouts of depression at one time or another.

THE PROPHET, ELIJAH

In 1 Kings 18-19, we see that because of the prophet Elijah's faith and obedience to God, his relationship with God was like few others, especially in his generation. God provided for him ravens for food when he was in the desert, he raised a boy from the dead, he had a standoff with a bunch of ungodly priests who dared to defy the one and only true God Jehovah, and his God backed him up with miracle after miracle, including sending down fire from heaven. You would think that someone with such a close walk with God would be immune to discouragement or depression, right? Wrong. Elijah was not immune. He was a mighty man of God, but he was human and had emotions that he had to sort out and fight through just like us. In fact, there was a wicked queen, Queen Jezebel who sent out a murderous decree for Elijah. Previously, he had killed all the false prophets of the land in Baal after they

OUR GOD OF PEACE

lost in a standoff against he and the one true God Jehovah. After hearing about the decree, however, Elijah spiraled into a depression so severe that he even asked God to take his life. It wasn't until God comforted him and he took the time to refocus on God's goodness and what He'd already done in his life that he properly dealt with the fear and other emotions he faced, refocused and put his confidence back in God. As always, God intervened on His behalf.

KING DAVID

The story of King David is a testament of God's love and redemption, but we also see how in the midst of David's sin and failures, he was extremely depressed because of his sins (2 Samuel 11:5-27). King David committed adultery, and he allowed his lust for another man's wife to consume him to the degree that he sent a woman's husband (Uriah) off to war to be killed just so that he could be with her. It wasn't until David admitted his sin that the depression (led on by sin) lifted.

> *When I kept silent about my sin, my body wasted away through my groaning all the day long. For day and night Your hand [of displeasure] was heavy upon me; my energy (vitality, strength) was drained away as with the burning heat of summer. Selah.* — **Psalm 32:3-4 AMP**

Cracked Mirrors

Do not cast me away from Your presence, And do not take Your Holy Spirit from me. Restore to me the joy of Your salvation, And uphold me by Your generous Spirit. Then I will teach transgressors Your ways, And sinners shall be converted to You. —**Psalm 51:11**

David even attributed the joy of God's salvation being taken away once he started walking in sin. The weight of our sins or past mistakes can be so overwhelming that we find we are unable to cope with our present situation. This is because sin separates us from God. If we were to look to God's Word in the midst of our sins, we'd see that the wages of our sins ultimately leads to death (Romans 6:23).

But now that you've found you don't have to listen to sin telling you what to do, and have discovered the delight of listening to God telling you, what a surprise! A whole, healed, put-together life right now, with more and more of life on the way! Work hard for sin your whole life and your pension is death. But God's gift is real, eternal life, delivered by Jesus, our Master. God is honest, pure, righteous and true, but He so desperately desires to help and restore us into right standing with Him. Unfortunately, many times we aren't inclined to run to God; when we slip up, we run away from God —**(Romans 3:23 The Message)**.

OUR GOD OF PEACE

Sometimes, what we may view as depression may actually be an imbalance of hormones as a result of a poor diet. Certain foods can trigger and make us prone to certain emotions that can influence us to react to or view situations in a skewed light. So be mindful, the Mirror warns us to be mindful of what we are putting in your body or temple (1 Corinthians 6:19). There's such a wealth of information available today on adopting a healthy diet and a good sleep and exercise regimen, so we have no excuse in this age of technology. Find out what works best for you, and again, pray to God for wisdom. He cares about every area of our lives including our health. When we are serving at our peak health, we are able to serve more effectively, think more soundly and accomplish the assignments God sends us on as we walk out our purpose.

FACING TRUTH

I have great news for you! Whether you choose to accept it or not, the truth is that it's our Father God's desire to take what is broken, unwanted and abused to not only make it as it was before it was broken but to restore beyond the original state, and it's all for His glory and honor! If you've been hurt by others, know that God heals and restores (Psalm 34:18). He is more than able. If you have fallen and have seemingly messed things up, rest assured that God forgives you the first time that you repent and ask

Cracked Mirrors

Him for forgiveness. He remembers your past sins no more. In fact, Micah 7:19 says, **"He will again have compassion on us, and will subdue our iniquities. He will cast all our sins into the depths of the sea."** So, contrary to what Satan may try to convince you of, God doesn't go back to boat's edge and dive back in trying to recover those sins that He already threw overboard. Once we repent and turn away from those sins, they are gone! So stop incessantly bringing up your past to God. It's no use: He doesn't remember it nor does He desire to.

While we may sit worried and perplexed about our lives and the future, God isn't shaken. He is our Rock (Psalm 95:1), and we can count on Him. He sits confident and unmoved by the circumstances in our lives because He is all knowing, all-powerful, and He holds time in His hands (Psalm 31:25). As a reminder, when we worry, we are telling God that we don't really trust Him. We don't whole-heartedly have faith in Him. So, as followers of Christ, we know that when we don't have faith in our God, it saddens Him — He isn't pleased. In fact, Hebrews 11:6 tells us that without faith, it is impossible to please God. We are really implying through our doubt in His character, that He is not a good Father and He doesn't really love us unconditionally.

Even as I was writing this book, God instructed me to write about the end from the beginning because He knows

OUR GOD OF PEACE

my past, present and future. He reassured me: "You are THE HEALED and the REDEEMED." I'm here to tell you as a witness that regardless of the fact that you are currently struggling with a condition, that you're out of money or supposedly out of time, if you follow Him and call Him your Father, then your so-called emotional state, feelings, negative bank account balance, or whatever the problem is, have no bearing on the Truth of His Word. God told me that the facts in my life are always subject to His Truth. So, as a result, I have peace. He has given us the "gift" of His peace.

John 14:27 NLT says, "I am leaving you with a gift—peace of mind and heart. And the peace I give is a gift the world cannot give. So don't be troubled or afraid."

In **Philippians 4:6-7** it says, "⁶ Be anxious for nothing, but in everything by prayer and supplication, with thanksgiving, let your requests be made known to God; ⁷ and the peace of God, which surpasses all understanding, will guard your hearts and minds through Christ Jesus." So, the truth be told, if we call God our Father, we have His promise that His peace will keep us.

Take a few moments and ask yourself, "Am I walking in the peace that God has given me?" If your answer is no, then now is the best time to enter into the rest that

Cracked Mirrors

God has already so freely given to you. It starts with trust. I want to encourage you to spend time *investing* in your relationship with God. Why use the word invest to describe your relationship with God? Because just like our earthly relationships, we get out of them what we put in. The best way to strengthen the trust that you have with someone is to spend time with them long enough to get to know them, their character, what they like or dislike. Sometimes, we find it difficult to really trust and have faith in God because we just haven't put the time into our relationship with Him. The truth is that we don't have difficulty trusting Him and His Word (the Mirror) because He has done something to abuse our trust; we have difficulty because we are unfamiliar with His character and as a result, we have challenges trusting Him. As you spend more time with Him, the easier it will become to rest in Him and His promises to you. He will never leave you nor forsake you, and you can take that to the bank. So, rest in Him now!

PRAYER TO THE FATHER:

"Father God, please forgive me for doubting You. I don't want to continue trusting in my own strength instead of placing confidence in You. Thank You so much for caring for me! I cast my burdens, worries and fears on You. I accept the peace that You have already made available to

OUR GOD OF PEACE

me. Thank You for continuing to teach me how to walk in Your peace and grace, in Jesus' Name. Amen."

Heart Reflections

Today, I learned / was reminded of:

_____
_____
_____
_____
_____
_____
_____
_____
_____
_____

With God's help, I will endeavor to work on:

_____
_____
_____
_____
_____
_____

It is important to confess over yourself WHO God says you are. Practice it now by looking in the mirror and confessing what God says about you. If you don't have a mirror, just use the mirror below, but visualize your reflection while you make these confessions over yourself.

- **I AM a doer of the Word, and I meditate on God's words daily.** (James 1:22, Joshua 1:8).
- **I am a new creature in Christ, old things have passed away, behold, all things are new.** (2 Corinthians 5:17)
- **I take every thought captive unto the obedience of Jesus Christ, casting down every imagination.** (Isaiah 54:17)
- **I know God's voice and a stranger's voice I do not recognize** (John 10:27).

Reflecting Christ's Image

HOW AM I LOOKIN'?

When people think about you, what are the first thoughts that they recall about you? Do they think lazy or ambitious? Lackadaisical or passionate? Faithful or unreliable? How do they perceive the quality of your body of work as an individual? While God does care about our heart, how the world and even your brothers and sisters in Christ view you is important to Him too because we are literally Christ's ambassadors here on earth (2 Corinthians 5:20).

We may miss the mark from time to time, but our heart should always be to live by a spirit of excellence. Do people know you as the person who embodies passion, poise and the gift of gab but lacks any form of the substance of commitment and follow-through regarding the things we proudly talk about? Whether we realize it or not, when we don't honor our word, our witness can begin to lose credibility in the eyes of our peers. It can possibly taint others' view of Christ, and after a while, it can open up the door to self-doubt. If we can't trust our own word, why should anyone else? We have all struggled with this at some point or another, but if this is something you are currently challenged with, I'd encourage you to go to God about it. First, ask Him for forgiveness for your misrepresenting Him, whether it was knowingly or not. Then ask Him to help you and show you any areas you need to improve on. Then commit to do better. If you are really serious about changing and making God proud, it doesn't matter how many times you may have fallen short in the past, through Christ, you will be victorious.

> *The godly may trip seven times, but they will get up again. But one disaster is enough to overthrow the wicked.* **—Proverbs 24:16**

> *For I can do everything through Christ, who gives me strength.* **—Philippians 4:13**

Whether its home life as a spouse, on the job or in ministry, give it your all and look for practical ways to

REFLECTING CHRIST'S IMAGE

better represent Christ so that He is getting the glory He is due. It's great to know Scripture and to be able to quote verses, but we have to be honest and ask ourselves if our work ethic truly mirrors the life of one that lacks discipline or one that is structured by it. Do you constantly arrive late to work? Are you slothful in your preparation for meetings? Things like these could be a potential hindrance to your witness if they're interpreted as a lack of character or commitment. None of us are perfect, but with God's help, we should be constantly striving for it or to become more like Him. Paul says in Philippians 3:12 that, "I don't mean to say that I have already achieved these things or that I have already reached perfection. But I press on to possess that perfection for which Christ Jesus first possessed me".

Again, in order to find out how we truly look in God's eyes and identify where we are in terms of following His precepts and maturing in Him, we must look at our Mirror, the Word of God.

> Imitate God, therefore, in everything you do, because you are his dear children. ² Live a life filled with love, following the example of Christ. He loved us and offered himself as a sacrifice for us, a pleasing aroma to God. ³ Let there be no sexual immorality, impurity, or greed among you. Such sins have no place among God's people. ⁴ Obscene stories, foolish talk, and

coarse jokes—these are not for you. Instead, let there be thankfulness to God. ⁵ You can be sure that no immoral, impure, or greedy person will inherit the Kingdom of Christ and of God. For a greedy person is an idolater, worshiping the things of this world. ⁶ Don't be fooled by those who try to excuse these sins, for the anger of God will fall on all who disobey him. ⁷ Don't participate in the things these people do. ⁸ For once you were full of darkness, but now you have light from the Lord. So live as people of light! ⁹ For this light within you produces only what is good and right and true.¹⁰ Carefully determine what pleases the Lord. ¹¹ Take no part in the worthless deeds of evil and darkness; instead, expose them. ¹² It is shameful even to talk about the things that ungodly people do in secret. ¹³ But their evil intentions will be exposed when the light shines on them, ¹⁴ for the light makes everything visible. This is why it is said,

—**Ephesians 5:1-14a**

CHRIST REPRESENTATIVES

In this last passage of Scripture, we can see that God's Word also encourages us to be imitators of Christ. Have you ever noticed how little children, during their infant years and well through toddler age, are just living, breathing human recorders? They watch everything. If it's a parent or a big sibling that they admire, they don't miss a beat trying to

REFLECTING CHRIST'S IMAGE

imitate everything that they see that parent or sibling do. Besides God's immaculate design of the human brain itself, research has shown that the brain actually doubles in size in the first year, and by age three it has reached 80 percent of its adult volume. (Urban Child Institute). That's truly remarkable! But, in addition to that though, I believe young children are able to absorb so much information because they are humble enough to just sit, watch, ask questions and practice what they see and/or hear for as long as it takes. Unlike most adults, the majority of time, they have no shame or pride that deters them from watching, emulating and learning what they desire to. What happens to us as adults where we lose that natural inclination to just sit, observe and learn? We sometimes struggle with humbling ourselves to admit that we are ignorant in certain areas and that perhaps, we could learn from one more knowledgeable. Adults often find it difficult just closing their mouths so that they are able to hear what it is they so desperately need to. Maybe that's why the apostle James encouraged us to remember to be slow to speak and quick to hear (James 1:19).

MENTORSHIP

In Matthew 18:1, we see that Jesus' disciples came to Him with the self-seeking question: "Who is greatest in the Kingdom of Heaven?" Jesus' response may have been puzzling to His followers at first. He tells them in the next two verses: "I tell you the truth, unless you turn from your sins and become like little children, you will never get into the Kingdom of Heaven. So anyone who becomes as humble as this little child is the greatest in the Kingdom of Heaven."

Jesus equated greatness to those who were humble as children. So, if we are Christ's ambassadors on this earth, and we want to improve the authenticity of our representation of Him, then one would assume that we would do our best to obey God's Word and mirror humility in our own lives. After all, how can we call ourselves followers of Christ if we are not following His example? Humility often lends to putting one's faith in someone that we hold in high esteem, even when we don't necessarily understand because we trust their wisdom, expertise and experience. It involves a submission of will despite intellect or emotion. If we desire to grow and mature spiritually, we must be diligent in our relationship with God through prayer, meditation and obedience so that as we look into the mirror of His Word, we allow Him to perfect those areas that concern us; where there is clear need for improvement. He doesn't expect us to do it on our own, but we must be humble enough to let Him know that we need His help. Along the way, it doesn't hurt to take advantage of the opportunity to be mentored by someone who has wisdom and has already been where you are going.

REFLECTING CHRIST'S IMAGE

BRAND JESUS

Part of my professional background is that of a graphic designer and brand specialist. I enjoy working with my clients, helping them to discover and craft their brand image and captivate their target audience. One way of accomplishing this is by developing a compelling brand story that communicates why they do what they do therein connecting them to their potential customers. A brand is simply "a unique design, sign, symbol, words, or a combination of these, employed in creating an image that identifies a product and differentiates it from its competitors. Over time, this image becomes associated with a level of credibility, quality, and satisfaction in the consumer's mind." Farmers have been using brands to identify and differentiate livestock for as long as we all can remember. Though it was viewed by some as inhumane, branding was once routinely performed with a hot iron on a visible part of the flesh of an animal. It seared a distinct image representing the owner of each animal so that there was no confusion about who owned what. The image on the cows on Farm A looked different than the image on the cows located on Farm B.

Brands don't just represent inanimate objects like computers, shoes and clothes; a person can also be referred to as a brand if they represent a unique image or reputation. You start associating certain people and things with a brand when there is a consistent representation of a look and feel, **values** or product performance upheld. If a brand consistently upholds what it advertises to others about itself, it is often described as a brand promise. Now, you may look at this as being deep, but even Jesus knew the importance of branding. In fact, in John 13:35, He actually tells his followers: By this, all will know that you are My disciples, if you have love for one another." LOVE was the *brand promise* that Jesus sought to be known by. He desired for the world to be able to clearly identify WHO belonged to Him. This agape love that Jesus was referring to distinguished Him from His competition -- the world and our enemy Satan. Time and time again throughout the Word of God, we see other references of "you'll know them by their fruit" (Matthew 7:20). This simply refers to the fact that you will identify a tree by the fruit that you see it bears. An apple tree will bear apples, and a plum tree will bear plums, not cucumbers. In a similar fashion, Jesus is telling us that we will be able to verify the authenticity of a person's character by the actions they carry out through their lifestyle.

Jesus's brand story was clear, and He clearly communicated His WHY or purpose to His disciples. You might even say that He delivered a *mini-elevator pitch* in John 3:16-17: [16]"For God so loved the world that He gave His only begotten Son, that whoever believes in Him

REFLECTING CHRIST'S IMAGE

should not perish but have everlasting life. [17] For God did not send His Son into the world to condemn the world, but that the world through Him might be saved."

Did you catch that? He tells us Who He and His Father are, what He is seeking to accomplish and why? This is because He wanted to make it absolutely clear to the world and to His followers who He was, what He represented and why He was there. In a similar fashion, God not only wants us to know about His love for us, He also wants the world to recognize us because we represent His brand -- Christianity. God is love. So, with God's help, we should do our absolute best to exemplify His love to others. It should radiate through our lifestyle and actions. You'll know them by their fruit (Matthew 7:15-20).

We should always have faith that God will bless the works of our hands as we grow and mature in Him. If we happen to fall short, it's always better if we commit to being our best while we make the necessary improvements. Remember: you are not a loser, so let's not think like losers. Always aim high and ask God to bless the works of your hands as you seek to honor Him as His representative. Properly representing Christ oftentimes requires both an attitude adjustment and a heart check, but are we strong enough mentally and spiritually to acknowledge weaknesses in our lives? We all have areas we can improve in, so that we can better represent Christ and reflect His love. We must never lose sight of the fact that our weaknesses can be opportunities for God to receive glory. Looking at 2 Corinthians 12:9 again, Paul says, "My grace is all you need. My power works best in weakness." So now I am glad to boast about my weaknesses, so that the power of Christ can work through me." We must remain humble throughout the process recognizing that one person's strength may be another's weakness and vice versa. The point is, we have to focus on ourselves, do some serious introspection and ask God to show us how we can better represent Him. In everything that we do, we should be faithful to God. Whether you're a gas station clerk, a construction worker or a bank executive, commit to being the best that you can be at your job and ask God to help you excel at it.

The master said, 'Well done, my good and faithful servant. You have been faithful in handling this small amount, so now I will give you many more responsibilities. Let's celebrate together! **—Matthew 25:23**

Sometimes, we can get discouraged along the way of stepping fully into our purpose because of our present circumstances. God may have revealed to you what He has called you to do, but maybe you're growing tired and frustrated, and you are ready to quit because you just

REFLECTING CHRIST'S IMAGE

don't understand how your present job or personal life situation quite falls in line with what you believe He has showed you. I want to encourage you to be patient and don't give up on the process. The Word of God encourages us to not grow weary in well doing (Galatians 6:9). It could be that God is simply preparing you for the next phase or assignment He is placing you on, but will you stay committed? Will you be diligent to learn during the process and take advantage of the experiences you've been graced to encounter? Will you continue to serve and work unto the Lord without murmuring and complaining? The condition of our hearts while we are serving or enduring through difficult seasons matters to God. All through the Word, we see one verse after another encouraging us to be content, and not murmur and complain.

> *For God is working in you, giving you the desire and the power to do what pleases him. Do everything without complaining and arguing, so that no one can criticize you. Live clean, innocent lives as children of God, shining like bright lights in a world full of crooked and perverse people.* — **Philippians 2:13-15**

> *Don't grumble about each other, brothers and sisters, or you will be judged. For look—the Judge is standing at the door!* —**James 5:9**

Cracked Mirrors

Not that I was ever in need, for I have learned how to be content with whatever I have. I know how to live on almost nothing or with everything. I have learned the secret of living in every situation, whether it is with a full stomach or empty, with plenty or little. For I can do everything through Christ, who gives me strength.
—Philippians 4:11-13

Never forget that you may be the only example of Jesus that people see. We should be jealous for the reputation of our loving God and for Him to receive the honor and reverence He is due. So, the next time you're tempted to half-do a job or under-perform because you're tired or lack the motivation to commit to what you gave your word to do, pause, reflect and ask yourself, "How am I lookin'? Does the level of commitment or work ethic that I'm demonstrating properly reflect the honor Christ is due?"

Heart Reflections

What image have I been portraying of Christ to family members and friends? What areas can I improve in? Go to your Heavenly Father about it.

_____

_____

REFLECTING CHRIST'S IMAGE

On the job and in business, what can I do to better represent Christ and a spirit of excellence so that God gets the glory He is due? Pray for wisdom and creativity in this area. God will answer you and honor your heart.

Reflections of:

MRS. ROSHANDA PRATT : *Wife, Mompreneur, faithful steward of 4, minister of the gospel, storyteller*

When you reflect on your image in the mirror, who do you see?
A strong, confident woman who understands the power of her voice and will not be silenced.

Summarize yourself prior to accepting Christ using 3 words:

Broken • Low Self-Esteem • Fearful

How does the viewpoint of the reflection that you see now differ from the person you were before your relationship with Christ? What's changed?
I realized on the other side of being born again that I was not worthless. Where I felt like a dead man walking, Christ has give me life. At one point I couldn't look at myself In the mirror without cringing. Now, I see the reflection of someone who is worthy not because of status, works but because God said so. What changed? My mind. The greatest decision one can make is to make a decision. The day I decided to receive Christ changed everything!

What was one of the most influential events in your life that influenced your perspective now or your relationship with Christ, as a whole?

I was in college and attending a women's conference and for the first time I could physical feel the love of God. I was overwhelmed by this love — a love I never knew was possible. From that day God has continued to capture my heart. With that kind of love, it has caused me to make decisions by God's grace that would bring fame to His name.

**How did God change your image?
Share in three words:**

Beautiful • Whole • Loved

"Before I formed you in the womb I knew you [and approved of you as My chosen instrument], And before you were born I consecrated you [to Myself as My own]; I have appointed you as a prophet to the nations." —**Jeremiah 1:5**

For Such a Time

FULFILLING YOUR GOD GIVEN PURPOSE

Growing up, a lot of children, especially boys, hear about or practice the camping trick of creating a fire using a mirror. In short, a mirror is used to reflect a strong beam of sunlight onto some type of fuel source like paper, grass or twigs. If the fuel source is held in one hand and aimed at the mirror under it in position where it is able to catch the sun's rays and directs them to the fuel source, then
— voila—a fire is started!

Did you know that God desires to light a fire in your heart that ignites a passion to pursue what He has created you to do? He has created YOU for such a time as this. By spending time in His face and meditating intently on the

Cracked Mirrors

Mirror of His Word, you'll notice a passion will start to stir inside of you. Your gifts, talents and abilities are needed right now. There is NO ONE on this earth that can fulfill the role, the purpose that God has created you to fulfill. So, why bother trying to fit into the shoes of someone else? I'm sorry to have to be the one to break it to you, but, there is no one that can successfully fulfill that role because God has blessed each of us with unique gifts (1 Peter 4:10-11).

The world needs you to be 100% of who GOD created you to be—not just 50% of you and the other half someone you may idolize or hold in high regard. The Bible says in Jeremiah 29:11, "I know the thoughts that I have of you. Thoughts to give you a future…" One of my favorite passages in the Bible is Jeremiah 1:5 AMP. Here, God is telling Jeremiah, "Before I formed you in the womb, I knew [and] approved of you [as my chosen instrument] and before you were born I separated and set you apart, consecrating you…" Can you believe it?! In like matter, God views you the same. You were set apart BEFORE you were even birthed out of your mother's womb. Just think about it: God loved you so much, and He cared so much about you that He took the time to carefully craft every intricate detail about you – both physically and intellectually, right down to your personality – EVERYTHING! Nothing was left undone. Take the time to study the Word of God and really get to know your Father and King. The more you

FOR SUCH A TIME

learn and embrace in your heart, the more difficult it will be for the enemy to dissuade you of God's thoughts of you and your purpose.

THE ULTIMATE DESIGNER

I enjoy the arts, as a whole. But regardless of how impressive I or anyone else may ever think of a design or campaign that I have created, it will always pale in comparison to the design skill set of the Giver of the Gifts. The God we serve is the ULTIMATE "designer". We can see this all throughout the Word of God, but let's just think on the plans that God gave Solomon for the construction of the Holy Tabernacle of Israel! It was God's desire for the temple to serve as a reflection of a holy domicile fit for the presence of our Almighty God to reside on earth. God literally "left no stone unturned". Check it out:

> [14] So Solomon finished building the Temple. [15] The entire inside, from floor to ceiling, was paneled with wood. He paneled the walls and ceilings with cedar, and he used planks of cypress for the floors. [16] He partitioned off an inner sanctuary—the Most Holy Place—at the far end of the Temple. It was 30 feet deep and was paneled with cedar from floor to ceiling. [17] The main room of the Temple, outside the Most Holy Place, was 60 feet long.
> [18] Cedar paneling completely covered the stone walls

Cracked Mirrors

throughout the Temple, and the paneling was decorated with carvings of gourds and open flowers.
—1 Kings 6:14-18

In the architectural plan for the Temple, there were details of gold, rubies, sapphire, onyx and all of the finest natural materials this world had to offer. Every color, fabric and stone was pre-selected before the construction. The exact dimensions for each panel and floor of the temple were given to Solomon. It's absolutely incredible the amount of detail that was taken even in the planning of this great work. So, the next time you get tempted to believe that God doesn't really care about the details of your life, stop and think on this. You can rest assured that He has already orchestrated down to the last detail, your purpose and each and every plan that He has for you.

THE AUTHOR OF TIME

Time has been defined by some as a measure in which events can be ordered, whether past, present or future. In Ecclesiastes 3:1, the Bible tells us, "To everything there is a season, and a time to every purpose under heaven." When studying the character of God, we see that He often moves and operates based on a pre-determined sequence. Oftentimes, our obedience is at the other end of us moving into a new season of time.

FOR SUCH A TIME

One of my favorite books of the Bible is Esther. By divine ordinance and some strategic planning orchestrated by THE ultimate Event Planner of all time, Esther was given the awesome opportunity of participating in the premiere beauty pageant in her country. Later God entrusted her with the influence to determine the fate of a nation!

Now, the winner of the contest Esther was a part of was to become the next queen to the king of Persia, Ahasuerus. I encourage you to read the entire book of Esther for yourself, if you haven't already, but just imagine a competition similar to the television series The Bachelor, where each of the potential new brides has a brief section of time to spend with the bachelor. He eventually makes his choice. Hopefully, you get the drift. Well, we see in verses 15-18 of chapter 2 that Esther was beautiful and her court decorum was impeccable, but through God, it was the favor and grace she obtained in the sight of the king that caused her to be selected to be the next queen of Persia.

HER DEFINING MOMENT

A little later in the story, we see that Esther was faced with a defining moment in her destiny. Esther was a Jew and at the time, there was an evil plot to wipe out all the Jews in the nation of Persia. Her people were in a predicament where without divine intervention, the Jewish nation could be totally annihilated! We don't know much about the details of Esther's upbringing, but we do know this: Esther was adopted. She had no parents, but she'd been raised by her uncle, Mordecai. He was her guardian and mentor. He helped to groom her the best he knew how. He was a faithful man of God and made sure Esther also knew his God. He saw the potential in her leading up to her competing in the pageant of the century. Throughout the story we can see how Esther trusted Mordecai's judgment. She eventually ended up winning the pageant and the king's heart.

THE CLOCK WAS COUNTING DOWN

Now, let's fast forward a bit. This leads us to the climax of the story. The clock was counting down, and we see that in spite of the favor that Esther feels she may have had in the past with the king, she is hesitant about approaching her now husband to request that the lives of God's people be spared. You see, in those days, it was customary for the king to allow individuals to enter into his presence when they were called. When they arrived, he would lift his golden scepter to them, signifying rite of passage. Those who came uninvited or who came at a time where the king did not desire his or her presence, risked an automatic death sentence. Ahasuerus had not called Esther into his chamber for a little while, so she battled fear at the thought of approaching him uninvited. Up until this point, Esther

FOR SUCH A TIME

had kept quiet about the fact that she was Jewish. So even though the Jewish people in the kingdom often felt hostility from the other inhabitants, it was easy for her, especially with her role in the kingdom, to avoid the hatred that her kinsman regularly faced. While Esther internally dealt with the uncomfortable decision, Mordecai - her mentor, her former trusted guardian, didn't let her off easy. He said in verse 14 of chapter 4:

Do not think in your heart that you will escape in the king's palace any more than all the other Jews. For if you remain completely silent at this time, relief and deliverance will arise for the Jews from another place, but you and your father's house will perish. Yet who knows whether you have come to the kingdom **for such a time as this**?

WOW? In God's divine providence, all the grooming, the months of preparation to even be considered to be the Queen of Persia, came down to this moment in time. I can imagine Esther gazing into her bedroom mirror in the royal palace. She's giving herself a pep talk: "You can do this. Uncle Mordecai is right. God has called me for such a time!" Esther had a decision to make. She could have taken the easy, more cowardly route and just looked out for her own interest. After all, no one would have been the wiser. Sure, she was a Jew, but if the plot to kill all her people had been carried out, no one could really blame her - it's all about survival of the fittest, right? Wrong. Esther's response was one of poise and courage - one truly fit for a queen — a daughter of Zion. She could have let the fact that she was adopted deter her from stepping into her purpose. Her relentless dependence on the God whom she believed had graced her with the opportunity to be in the position she now held, motivated her to fast and pray for direction and through her uncle, she'd also asked the other Jews in the nation to pray as well.

She said: "Go and gather together all the Jews of Susa and fast for me. Do not eat or drink for three days, night or day. My maids and I will do the same. And then, though it is against the law, I will go in to see the king. If I must die, I must die." (Esther 4:15)

In the next three chapters of Esther, we see that God answers in her favor - as only He can! Through Esther's courage to approach the king, God moved on His heart to extend favor to her and all her people. Again, I encourage you to read the entire story, but to summarize the ending of the story: the evil plot to destroy the Jews was exposed and the destiny of the nation of Israel was altered greatly through one woman's obedience. As a result, God delivered His people from extinction and prospered the country, as a whole.

FOR SUCH A TIME

WHAT ABOUT ME?

So, you may say, "Yeah, great story, but what does Queen Esther have to do with me?" Well, think about it: we each have been faced with or will face our own *defining moments* in time. That job, that project, that pressing family situation...not only do the decisions that we make on a daily basis affect our today and tomorrow, but they often affect others indirectly in a greater magnitude than we could imagine. God doesn't show us all the pieces of the puzzle at the beginning because we'd most likely lose heart just trying to connect the dots and make sense of it all. God expects us to have faith and obey Him with the first set of instructions He has given us. Once we walk in obedience, He gives us the next set of instructions.

Oftentimes, people will try to place their own value on individuals based on their upbringing, bank account, their looks, so-called natural gifts and abilities or social status. It is just human nature to ridicule, critique or underestimate what one does not understand. However, God makes it clear that He doesn't consider the outward appearance of a person at all when determining whether they are qualified to accomplish the purpose that He has assigned them. He doesn't revisit your past or consult with the opinions of man to see whether or not you are fit to fulfill what He has already ordained for your life. Where man is caught up looking at the external makeup, God is only concerned with that person's heart (1 Samuel 16:4-13). Many times, God may look right over individuals who on paper appear to be qualified to accomplish His will and instead use the so-called nobody, the person that everyone had already counted out as useless or a failure. While we cannot attempt to understand all of God's ways, we do know that He uses foolish things to confound the wise and weak vessels to shame those that are powerful (1 Corinthians 1:27). This is because God gets the glory when all can see that it is He and not the vessel that has accomplished a task. We should be grateful for the opportunity to be used as God's vessel because each time He uses us, His glory reflects off of us and on to others. Don't be concerned about any flaws, idiosyncrasies or any other so-called weaknesses while serving God and obeying what He has called you to. Not only is God's power best demonstrated in weakness (2 Corinthians 12:9), but it's an absolute honor and joy to be used and walking in what God has called you to. Don't be concerned or discouraged if people look at you disapprovingly because you don't measure up to their standards of what God's vessel should look or sound like. They may say that you're too big, too small, too thin, your voice is too deep, your voice is too high, you stutter, you have a limp, your hair's too kinky, your hair's too straight, you have no hair, you have a record, you're too dark, too pale, you're not intellectual enough, your eyes are too big,

FOR SUCH A TIME

you don't fit in their clique or whatever - but who cares?! You are *God's vessel*, not theirs, so their opinion on what belongs to God is totally irrelevant. Never lose sight of the privilege it is to serve such a great God. Continue to go to and reflect in His Mirror for validation. Always trust and obey His Word and thank Him for His strength as you grow closer in your walk with Him.

It is important to confess over yourself WHO God says you are. Practice it now by looking in the mirror and confessing what God says about you. If you don't have a mirror, just use the mirror below, but visualize your reflection while you make these confessions over yourself.

- **I AM unique and fearfully & wonderfully made.** (Psalm 139:14).
- **God's plans for me are good! He desires to prosper me as I seek Him.** (Jeremiah 29:11)
- **Whatever I put my hand to prospers; God has prospered me in every area of my life**. (John 10:3-5; 14-16, 27; John 14:15)
- I refuse to walk in hate or unforgiveness. (1 John 2:11; Ephesians 4:32)

Using Cracked Mirrors

In the past, I have struggled with being slow to obey or step out into what God has called me to walk in. A lot of this was because I'd try to analyze every little thing throughout the process in my faith walk. God would show me bits and pieces and give me instructions to move on, and in my heart, I knew that He had confirmed His Word, but I'd try to get clarity on any gray areas before totally stepping out. **That's not faith.** By the grace of God, I've improved in this and am still growing, but I have to tell you that faith is stepping out into the unseen before you quite know what the next step is. Faith is not an excuse to not use wisdom nor is it going through life making irresponsible decisions. You can always go to God for wisdom if you are unclear on a matter, but when God speaks to you and gives you instructions, it's your responsibility to obey.

> *Faith shows the reality of what we hope for; it is the evidence of things we cannot see.* —**Hebrews 11:1**

It is impossible for us to please God without faith (Hebrews 11:6). Faith in God grows out of a total reliance in Him and His Word, regardless of what things may look like around you or how you may feel or think. The more we build our relationship with God by spending time with Him and reflecting on what He has to say about things, the more our confidence deepens in His character. God is not like man, so He cannot lie. Whatever He has promised you, He will carry it out and fulfill it in your life (Numbers 23:19).

So, don't wait! Pursue your dreams & visions. The next time you think of that business idea or that book manuscript that's been literally "sitting on the shelf", ask yourself how many people could have been impacted for the good had you only been diligent in your pursuit? Ask God how He desires for you to use your gifts and talents. First, I'd recommend that you establish a relationship with your Creator, if you haven't already, because there's no one who knows you better than your Creator. Accept Jesus Christ into your heart. He loves you unconditionally, and this way, you can find out what His divine purpose is for your life. Trust me: it's the

USING CRACKED MIRRORS

greatest way to live and be fulfilled in life.

Since God created you and formed you in your mother's womb, it's a pretty fair assumption that no one truly is more schooled and knowledgeable of your inner workings — your thoughts, emotions, gifts, aspirations and fears than the One who is omniscient. So, don't grow weary or frustrated if you're not sure exactly what you were called to do. God is faithful, and He desires to reveal your purpose to you, but He wants you to have faith in Him and trust that the Father knows best. He will speak to your heart and make it clear to you; just rest in Him. Sometimes, we may feel pressured to cave in and pursue things that are not in God's plan for us because they are careers or pursuits that are popular or viewed as successful life goals by the world's standards. You may come from a family with a long history of medical professionals, but in your heart of hearts, you just feel that your gifts and desires are calling you in a totally different direction. Or maybe you came from a family where not much good was expected of you. If that's you, no matter how your family, peers or even friends try to influence you, rest assured that your Father truly does know what is best for you. He believes in you and so do I! Be brave enough to stand up for what you feel God has called you to do and be. Pray for God's strength in this area, and He will give it to you.

Spending time in our Father's presence and praying in

Reflections of:

MS. TIA JONES : *26 year old young woman, faithful Army vet, who is currently a full time college student*

When you reflect on your image in the mirror, who do you see?
I see a strong woman who is full of purpose. I also see worth, value, and beauty.

Summarize yourself prior to accepting Christ using 3 words:

Worthless • Fearful • Hopeless

How does the viewpoint of the reflection that you see now differ from the person you were before your relationship with Christ? What's changed?
Now that I have a relationship with Christ and know Him as my Savior, I no longer identify myself by my painful experiences. Instead, I've found my identity, worth, value, and security in what God's love for me, and what He has done for me on the cross. I turned from searching for healing, value, hope, security, and love in ungodly relationships/ friendships and pursued God.

What was one of the most influential events in your life that influenced your

perspective now or your relationship with Christ, as a whole?

Internally, I held onto deep, childhood wounds for years. These were the wounds I thought no one cared about due to the experience of abandonment. When I first gave my life to God, I asked if He could show me that He cared about me. Not too long after that, He sent people to speak into my life. God sent them to answer the prayer that I prayed to Him. Since then, I knew that God cared about me. I learned that God noticed me and the pain that I experienced.

**How did God change your image?
Share in three words:**
Valuable • Secure • Loved

the Holy Spirit will stir up the gift inside of you (2 Timothy 1:6). The more you adapt this lifestyle, the more in sync you will become with the will of God. When you're in tune with God, it becomes easier to hear God's voice and understand His instructions as you pursue His calling on your life.

STEPPING OUT OF COMFORT ZONES

In the book of Exodus in the Bible, we see that God's people, the Hebrews, were living in a horrible state of slavery and captivity at the hands of the Egyptians. They suffered grueling hours of abuse and oppression. Moses was actually on the run, because he had killed a cruel Egyptian taskmaster that he saw abusing one of the Hebrew slaves. Word got out about the murder, and he had to flee. God spoke to the prophet Moses from within a burning bush, which was a miracle in itself. He revealed to him that he was called to lead the children of Israel out of the captivity of the Egyptians, but he struggled with the call.

In Exodus 4:10-12 NLT, we see: [10]"But Moses pleaded with the Lord, **"O Lord, I'm not very good with words. I never have been, and I'm not now,** even though you have spoken to me. I get tongue-tied, and my words get tangled." [11] Then the Lord asked Moses, "Who makes a person's mouth? Who decides whether people speak or do not speak, hear or do not hear, see or do not see? Is it not I,

USING CRACKED MIRRORS

the Lord? [12] Now go! I will be with you as you speak, and I will instruct you in what to say."

Moses struggled with obeying God because his public speaking skills were not the best. In fact, he felt completely inadequate to fulfill the assignment God had given him. I mean, how could he be expected to lead God's people out of Egypt? He could barely speak without his words getting all twisted up, so Moses tried to reject the call of God. Can you relate? Do you also feel completely inadequate? Are the true desires and passions of your heart somehow leading you in a different direction than your intellect because they would demand that you journey out of your comfort zone? Moses was clearly called by God and given specific instructions to lead His people out of the land of Egypt, but Moses failed to realize that before God called him, He was already aware of His so-called physical limitations. Long story short, once Moses submitted his thoughts and wills to God and obeyed Him, God used him lead His people out of the land of Egypt and towards God's Promised Land for them. He did this all, in spite of, His initial fear and speech impediment earlier on.

Oftentimes, our fears and insecurities cause us to offer God questions and rebuttals that are actually really insults to His character when you think about it. Again, God is not a man that He should lie (Numbers 23:19); and because He knows all things, He is already aware of any so-called weaknesses and flaws that we may possess before He reveals our calling and purpose. When God calls us to do something, we can rest assured that He already knows who He called and what weaknesses may come along with that vessel. Growth, victory and the goals that we pursue can often be obtained once we gain the courage to venture outside of the confines of our comfort zones. Make it a habit to obey Him promptly. God is a God of timing. He will provide what is needed to fulfill the assignment. In fact, in 2 Corinthians 12:9 NLT, Paul asked God on multiple occasions to remove the "thorn in his flesh", and God replied to Him: "My grace is all you need. My power works best in weakness." This revelation blessed Paul and he responded, "So now I am glad to boast about my weaknesses, so that the power of Christ can work through me." When you are truly walking in your purpose, you will be the happiest and most fulfilled because you are doing what you were created to do.

Don't be stressed because you don't understand how it all is going to come together. Just have faith and trust in God that He knows best, and He will provide. Never forget that your purpose is not just about you. It's all about what God wants to do through you, and you can rest assured that His will and your purpose will always include helping others in some way. It's always for His honor and glory. So, don't allow fear or the opinions of yourself or others to rob

USING CRACKED MIRRORS

you of your destiny. If you're still a bit unsure of what God's plans are for your life, take it to God and seek Him with all your heart. He will reveal and confirm your purpose to you (Hebrews 11:6). Also, seek wise counsel, like your pastor, a parent, guardian, good friend or even a relative that may know you well enough to be able to see what areas you are gifted in. Then, if the counsel given to you matches up with what's in your heart, take it back to God for instructions on the next steps. Trust Him to work out the details.

WHO DO YOU THINK YOU ARE, ANYWAY?

In one account in the Bible, Philip identified Jesus by telling the others: "We have found the very person Moses and the prophets wrote about! His name is Jesus, the son of Joseph from Nazareth." (John 1:43-50). However, when Nathanael heard this, his immediate response was, **"Can anything good come from Nazareth?"** Phillip simply told him, "Come and see for yourself". Wow! Nathanael pretty much just dissed Jesus. You see, in that day and age, Nazareth of Galilee was probably a village of no more than 500 in the days when Jesus grew up there. In today's time, it would probably be described as "the backwoods" or "out in the sticks". So, some of the more educated and urban Jews thought that the Nazarenes were ignorant, simple-minded and not well versed in the doctrine of Judaism. However, later in the chapter, Jesus reveals to

Cracked Mirrors

Nathanael his happenings earlier that day even down to the location of the tree that he had sat under. It's clearly evident to him that he is not dealing with just any run-of-the mill Jew. What's my point? You may be completely elated about God's revealing His purpose for your life, but that doesn't mean others will be. In fact, other people — friends, family members and associates may not even believe in you or what God has called you to do. As you step out in faith and out of your comfort zone, you're going to find that you may have to tune out the opinions of those around you like never before. In Matthew 7:6, God instructs us not to cast our pearls before swine. The plans that our God reveals to us for our life do not require the approval of man, who is frail as breath (Isaiah 2:22). It doesn't matter that others don't believe or trust you. We ought to be more concerned with obeying and doing the will of our Father than we are getting with the approval from those with vacillating opinions of us — and sometimes even themselves. God knows best, and He sees the end from the beginning. There's a reason why the psalmist in the book of Proverbs wrote to put our confidence in God rather than our own intellect:

> [5] Trust in and rely confidently on the Lord with all your heart And do not rely on your own insight or understanding. [6] In all your ways know and acknowledge and recognize Him, And He will make your paths straight

USING CRACKED MIRRORS

and smooth [removing obstacles that block your way]. ⁷ Do not be wise in your own eyes; Fear the Lord [with reverent awe and obedience] and turn [entirely] away from evil. —**Proverbs 3:5-7 AMP**

There will come a time, if you haven't experienced it already, that you will face someone doubting your abilities or competency. Again, they may be skeptical of the vision that you believe that God has called you to because you may not appear to fit the mold of everyone else around you. Go back to the Mirror and remind yourself Who God says you are. He delights in using materials that man would have otherwise regarded as useless, purposeless and futile to build masterpieces. He gets the glory when a vessel that is considered weak and incapable is used to accomplish a mighty feat (1 Corinthians 1:27). The truth is, we can't afford to hold the opinions of others on a higher pedestal than God's opinion and instructions to us unless we're willing to risk foregoing our God-given destiny. Get and stay focused. Don't entertain negativity. You have a divine purpose and calling, so don't let anyone discourage you from pursuing it by reminding you of your past, failures and flaws. If you even need to tell them verbally, you remind them of what God's word says: "I can do ALL things through Christ who strengthens me." — Philippians 4:13

So, I want you to encourage you again: if you've been

counted out or overlooked by man simply because you don't fit the physical build to accomplish what God has called you to accomplish, don't be dismayed. Welcome to the club — Club X. The club for the discounted, overlooked, seemingly unpolished, unqualified and inadequate. Maybe you feel like your name has been crossed off the list of potentials to ever be successful and fulfilled, and instead transferred to the list for those who have already been determined as not enough. Everyone may have already written you off as unusable to accomplish anything worthwhile. Well that "x" need not serve as a mark of shame any longer in your life. God has branded you and set you apart for His will and purpose. He loves you, and He delights in using men and women who are obedient and have faith in God to fulfill His will. You were built for greatness. Remember: no more cracks! God has healed you and restored you. Your past has been forgiven and God remembers it no more. Keep looking into His Mirror for validation. His stamp of approval on you is all the endorsement you need to step into your purpose.

GOD IS COUNTING ON YOU

Our world is constantly advancing, but God's Word is forever settled in heaven (Psalm 119:89). Regardless of how intelligent mankind may feel they are, their knowledge will always pale in comparison to their Creator. With

USING CRACKED MIRRORS

everything that is going on in our society, opposing views about morality and the value of life itself, the line has been drawn in the sand. Gone are the days to straddle the fence in our beliefs. As Moses infamously said to the children of Israel in Exodus 32:26, when there were two opposing views in the camp: "Whoever is for the LORD, come to me." And all the Levites rallied to him." We love people with the love of God, but because we love them, we have to lovingly speak the truth to them about God's views on lifestyles and sins that are not pleasing to Him because sin separates God and man. When your image in the eyes of the world surpasses the importance of what you see in the Mirror of the Word of God, destruction will soon follow.

STOP — THERE'S A CLIFF AHEAD!

Just imagine you're outside hiking, enjoying the beautiful spring weather. You breathe in deeply to take in the fresh mountain air and smile with the soft crunch of the golden leaves under your feet. You finished your hike but, as you turn around to make your way back down the hiking path, in your peripheral vision, you see motion. You stop abruptly to see what it is, when you notice a friend of yours running full speed down a hill, but instead of rearing to the right where you are, they are headed directly towards a hidden embankment that leads towards the edge of a cliff. What would you do? You realize that you don't have enough time to explain things to them but that you could probably block their path or get their attention if you move quickly enough. So, without thinking about it further, you dart like a fiery cannon in their direction to divert their path and...BOOM! The two of you collide, and they are hurled to the ground and down, just short of the edge of the cliff. They get up slowly and glare up at you, half upset and partly confused. You think to yourself, "Whew! That was close, but MISSION ACCOMPLISHED". A little disshoveled, you dust yourself off and stand up with a slight sense of pride. I mean, after all, you just saved the day, right? Uh...no. Your friend is not so thrilled. As far as they are concerned, not only did you just interrupt their morning run by darting directly in their path and into their torso, the collision they just sustained also caused them to lose their breakfast in the process. For a moment, they glare at you because of the temporary discomfort they just experienced and think to themselves, "Clumsy fool! Why weren't you looking where you were going anyway?!" However, once you fully explain what really happened, and they have a chance to evaluate the casualty they just avoided, their stare softens, and they are reduced to tears of gratitude. Why the abrupt change in attitude? This is because they realize the complexity of the situation and that you valued them and cared for their lives enough to risk them being temporarily irritated or hurt by you.

USING CRACKED MIRRORS

This may have seemed like a long-winded, colorful tale, but in a way it's an allegorical representation of what many Christians seem to struggle with regularly in terms of sharing the Love of God . Instead of sounding the alarm, we let family, friends, loved ones and strangers sprint head first right off the deep embankment and don't say a peep to them for fear of risking their being temporarily disenchanted with our presenting them with the Truth of the Gospel. Some of our friends or family members don't have a relationship with Christ. Are we allowing our discomfort from their rejection of Christ to dissuade us from sharing the love of God with them? Yes, the Truth will be unsettling and even jolting to some because darkness and light cannot co-exist, but we are called to walk in light (Ephesians 5:8-11).

GOD NEEDS YOU

You and I are living in the last of the last days. Jesus is returning back for His Church soon, and it's imperative that we be about our Father's business, sharing the Good News and walking in the calling that God has placed on our lives. Let's be real. Think about it: how many of your friends or family members are on their way to hell because they don't know our Lord and Savior, Jesus Christ? How many of them are suffering from depression, negative self-images and living in bondage to sin, when we have the answer?! JESUS is the answer.

Cracked Mirrors

Everyone may not be called into the five-fold ministry (Ephesians 4:11-12), but we have all been assigned by God with the responsibility to always be ready to give a reason for the hope that we find in Jesus (see 1 Peter 3:15). We have to be more concerned about the permanent spiritual death that those who don't come into a relationship with Christ will suffer in hell, then we are about being accepted or liked by others temporarily. You may feel this statement to be strong, but how will your loved one really feel about you if they are banished to hell, and you are sent to heaven, after they realize you could have saved them by simply opening up your mouth to share the Truth with them? God has called us to tell others about the Good News of the Gospel. (If you do not yet have a relationship with Christ, it's important that you realize that hell was never designed for man. It was designed for Satan and the other fallen angels. However, once Adam sinned in the Garden of Eden, mankind was separated spiritually from God because of sin. God loved us so much though, He sent His Son Jesus to be a ransom for us. Jesus is the bridge that leads us back to God, and He wants us to share His love with all of mankind.) God may call us to plant seed by telling someone about Christ and other times, they may accept Him on the spot. We are God's ambassadors — his representatives here on earth. We are His hands and feet, and He has called you for such a time as this to share His

USING CRACKED MIRRORS

love to this lost and dying world. God has been so faithful to us, so let's not let Him down because we are ashamed of Him, when He gave His all so freely for us so that we could be saved from eternal damnation.

PRAYER TO THE FATHER:

Father God, I know that You love me. So much so that You took the time to catalog the very hairs of my head. I will not be bitter or resentful to those who have hurt me in the past. I've forgiven them, and You have completely healed me emotionally. I am whole in You. I declare today, Father God, that I will move forward into the purpose You have called me to using the gifts and talents that You have blessed me with. God, I accept the reality that You have completely healed and restored my formerly broken heart. I am a NEW man/woman! I am more than a conqueror!

I want to encourage you to be both proactive and aggressive in strengthening your relationship with Christ. Fight fear; fight laziness; fight self-doubt. Confess the Word over yourself and your emotions daily, and be intentional about spending time with Him, so that you can grow in your walk with Him and remain sensitive to His spirit and gentle promptings. God pursued us despite the self-rejection or failures of the past. He loves us unconditionally and always will. He's redeemed us and set us free — free to pursue our

Cracked Mirrors

dreams and His purpose for our lives. We really can trust in Him that He will complete the work He has started in us! Because God is with us, we have nothing to fear. God is counting on you to keep moving forward.

I believe in you and that you will be successful and accomplish all that God has placed on your heart as you keep your confidence in Him. Always remember to keep your eyes on Him, steady on His loving reflection of you. Let your self-worth forever mirror the value that God has already placed on your life and dictated in the Mirror of the Word of God. He will NEVER leave you or forsake you all the days of your life. He desires for your reflection to be clarified in His glory and for your cracked mirror to be mended and bonded with His everlasting love for you. In the mighty Name of Jesus, you will never be the same.

Always remember to stay close to His Mirror.

**TRUST GOD. DREAM BIG.
YOU ARE CALLED.
FOR SUCH A TIME.**

Author Bio

Tiara Cloud is passionate about encouraging others to pursue their God given gifts, talents and abilities "for such as a time". In addition to serving in various outreach opportunities within her community over the last decade, she is also the founder of For Such A Time, an organization that offers unique stationery, gifts & timely encouragement to the recipients. She holds a Bachelor of Arts degree in Graphic Arts over 15 years of experience in brand development, graphic arts and web design. She also serves as an instructor at More Than Conquerors College in Charlotte, NC.

Tiara's Encoura-Card collection, an inspirational line of greeting cards containing uplifting messages intended to bring both encouragement and a smile to the face of each recipient has been featured on NBC's WCNC *Charlotte Today* show. For information on upcoming events or projects, please visit the website below or follow Tiara on social media at the links below:

facebook.com/itsforsuchatime
instagram.com/itsforsuchatime
forsuchatime.today

Helpful Resources

If you do not know Jesus as your Savior and Lord, simply pray the following prayer in faith, and He will be your Lord!

PRAYER FOR SALVATION

Heavenly Father, I come to You in the Name of Jesus. Your Word says, "Whosoever shall call on the name of the Lord shall be saved" (Acts 2:21). I am calling on You. I pray and ask Jesus to come into my heart and be Lord over my life according to Romans 10:9-10: "⁹ If you openly declare that Jesus is Lord and believe in your heart that God raised him from the dead, you will be saved. ¹⁰ For it is by believing in your heart that you are made right with God, and it is by openly declaring your faith that you are saved." I do that now. I confess that Jesus is Lord, and I believe in my heart that God raised Him from the dead.

I am now reborn! I am a Christian—a child of Almighty God! I am saved! You also said in Your Word, "If ye then being evil, know how to give good gifts unto your children: HOW MUCH MORE shall your heavenly Father give the Holy Spirit to them that ask him?" (Luke 11:13) I'm also asking You to fill me with the Holy Spirit. Holy Spirit, rise up within me as I praise God. I fully expect to speak with other tongues as You give me the utterance (Acts 2:4).
In Jesus' Name. Amen.

Other Resources

FOR SUCH A TIME

"For if you remain completely silent at this time, relief and deliverance will arise for the Jews from another place, but you and your father's house will perish. Yet who knows whether you have come to the kingdom for such a time as this?" —**Esther 4:14**

Part of the mission of **For Such A Time** is to offer encouragement while sharing the love of God through the use of beautiful, uplifting printed products such as stationery, including greeting and note cards, gift boxes, custom gift bags, handmade crafts and more! We believe that the products designed are a tool to reach individuals in their time of need "for such a time as this".

We've endeavored to partner with a number of organizations whose missions are aligned with ours with the donation of certain products to encourage their own program participants.

It is the goal of **For Such A Time** to encourage individuals to pursue their God given gifts, talents and abilities "for such as a time".

TAKE THE TIME TO JOT A LINE WRITING CAMPAIGN

The **Take the Time to Jot a Line Campaign** serves as a means to encourage those who are facing difficult times or those who are in the need of encouragement. It provides a platform for those who would like to make an impact in the lives of those in need, to take the time to do so. Several psychologists / scientists believe that writing actually promotes memory formation, which is why several schools and parents have pushed for their students to implement handwriting in curricula more regularly. For Such A Time supports this initiative through its "Take the Time to Jot a Line" Campaign. This campaign can be implemented into the curriculum of schools whose objectives include promoting handwriting and literacy.

FUTURE CAMPAIGN TYPES (card writing party)
- **SERVICE:** for distribution to U.S. Service men and women & Veterans
- **SURVIVORS:** written to domestic violence survivors, human trafficking victims / survivors to be coupled with other care packages given by partner organizations
- **GRATITUDE:** for personal use
- **EDUCATION:** partnership with local schools to help promote handwriting

If you are interested in helping to host a writing campaign, please visit forsuchatime.today or call 704-287-2409.

Let us know how Cracked Mirrors has impacted your life! We would love to hear from you. Drop us a line to let us know at forsuchatime.today.

www.ingramcontent.com/pod-product-compliance
Lightning Source LLC
LaVergne TN
LVHW051521070426
835507LV00023B/3229